A Comprehensive Critique of Student Evaluation of Teaching

This thought-provoking volume offers a comprehensive analysis of contemporary research and literature on student evaluation of teaching (SET) in Higher Education.

In evaluating data from fields including education, psychology, engineering, science, and business, this volume critically engages with the assumption that SET is a reliable and valid measure of effective teaching. Clayson navigates a range of cultural, social, and era-related factors including gender, grades, personality, student honesty, and halo effects to consider how these may impact on the accuracy and impartiality of student evaluations. Ultimately, he posits a "popularity hypothesis," asserting that above all, SET measures instructor likability. While controversial, the hypothesis powerfully and persuasively draws on extensive and divergent literature to offer new and salient insights regarding the growing and potentially misleading phenomenon of SET.

This topical and transdisciplinary book will be of great interest to researchers, faculty, and administrators in the fields of higher-education management, administration, teaching, and learning.

Dennis E. Clayson is Professor Emeritus at the University of Northern Iowa, USA, and has taken degrees in both physics and experimental psychology. He has been active in perceptual studies and in the pragmatic application of marketing research. He became interested in the student evaluation of teaching over 30 years ago after being asked by college administrators to investigate the process. His extensive work on the evaluations has been widely cited.

Routledge Research in Higher Education

Developing and Utilizing Employability Capitals
Graduates' Strategies across Labour Markets
Edited by Tran Le Huu Nghia, Thanh Pham, Michael Tomlinson, Karen Medica and Christopher D. Thompson

The Dispositif of the University Reform
The Higher Education Policy Discourse in Poland
Helena Ostrowicka, Justyna Spychalska-Stasiak and Łukasz Stankiewicz

Teacher Education at Hispanic-Serving Institutions
Exploring Identity, Practice, and Culture
Edited by Janine M. Schall, Patricia Alvarez McHatton, Eugenio Longoria Sáenz

Graduate Research Supervision in the Developing World
Policies, Pedagogies, and Practices
Edited by Erik Blair, Danielle Watson and Shikha Raturi

Posthuman and Political Care Ethics for Reconfiguring Higher Education Pedagogies
Edited by Vivienne Bozalek, Michalinos Zembylas and Joan C. Tronto

A Comprehensive Critique of Student Evaluation of Teaching
Critical Perspectives on Validity, Reliability, and Impartiality
Dennis E. Clayson

Community Engagement in Christian Higher Education
Enacting Institutional Mission for the Public Good
Edited by P. Jesse Rine and Sandra Quiñones

For more information about this series, please visit: www.routledge.com/Routledge-Research-in-Higher-Education/book-series/RRHE

A Comprehensive Critique of Student Evaluation of Teaching
Critical Perspectives on Validity, Reliability, and Impartiality

Dennis E. Clayson

Routledge
Taylor & Francis Group
NEW YORK AND LONDON

First published 2021
by Routledge
52 Vanderbilt Avenue, New York, NY 10017

and by Routledge
2 Park Square, Milton Park, Abingdon, Oxon, OX14 4RN

Routledge is an imprint of the Taylor & Francis Group, an informa business

© 2021 Dennis E. Clayson

The right of Dennis E. Clayson to be identified as authors of this work has been asserted by him in accordance with sections 77 and 78 of the Copyright, Designs and Patents Act 1988.

All rights reserved. No part of this book may be reprinted or reproduced or utilised in any form or by any electronic, mechanical, or other means, now known or hereafter invented, including photocopying and recording, or in any information storage or retrieval system, without permission in writing from the publishers.

Trademark notice: Product or corporate names may be trademarks or registered trademarks, and are used only for identification and explanation without intent to infringe.

Library of Congress Cataloging-in-Publication Data
A catalog record for this title has been requested

ISBN: 978-0-367-54984-8 (hbk)
ISBN: 978-1-003-09146-2 (ebk)

Typeset in Times New Roman
by Apex CoVantage, LLC

Do not pay attention to every word people say, or you may hear your servant cursing you – for you know in your heart that many times you yourself have cursed others.

Ecclesiastes 7: 21–22

Contents

1. Issues and Debates Surrounding Student Evaluations of Teaching ... 1
2. Potential Impacts of Gender Bias on Student Evaluations ... 13
3. The Influence of Personality Traits on Student Evaluations ... 23
4. Halo Effects Impacting on Student Evaluations ... 31
5. Are Students Truthful? ... 44
6. Rigor, Grades, and How They Impact Student Evaluations ... 49
7. The Association Between Student Learning and Student Evaluations ... 64
8. Student Evaluations and the Improvement of Instruction ... 74
9. Challenging the Statistical Reliability of Student Evaluations ... 81
10. Traditional Validity and SET ... 87
11. Identifying Valid Applications of SET ... 103

12	Validity and the Impacts of Subjectivity	112
13	Introducing a Likability Hypothesis	122
14	Justifications of the Likability Hypothesis	133
15	Conclusion and Recommendations – the Future of SET	144

Index 147

1 Issues and Debates Surrounding Student Evaluations of Teaching

What Are the Issues?

Louis thought of himself as a good teacher. He also loved research. These two passions were what led him to become a professor. Even as an undergraduate, he found he could explain things to his classmates so they readily understood them. Numerous times, someone he helped would say, "Why didn't the professor explain it like that?" Upon gaining his doctorate, Louis went to work for a private college where he enjoyed his interaction with students, and felt pride in their achievements. Yet, in the second decade of teaching, Louis saw his student evaluations go from the top 90th percentile to the bottom 20th percentile. In other words, he, in the eyes of his students, went from one of the best instructors to one of the worst. What could have caused such a dramatic reversal? The only change in Louis's life was a change in schools. He left the private school where he had taught for almost ten years for a larger public university, which increased his salary and gave him more opportunities for research. Prior to his move, he was twice nominated by graduating seniors for the college's faculty award, the highest honor given by the college to faculty. In his last year, he was nominated by his peers to give the faculty lecture, another honor, this time by his colleagues. After his first year at the new university, he was shocked to find his student evaluations were lower than he had ever experienced. Years later, his scores remained below average. Louis became convinced there was something wrong with the evaluation process. His approach in the classroom had not changed. His personality and his ability to explain complicated material had not been suddenly modified. He knew his students were different, but were they that much different? They were all undergraduate students. Nothing he had done had created this change, so what was the evaluation actually measuring? Was he a good teacher or was he not? Where once Louis couldn't wait to get into the classroom, he now dreaded each new class.

2 Issues and Debates Surrounding SET

What can we tell Louis? Were the evaluations his students completed almost every term assessing his actual teaching ability? If not, then what were they measuring? Perhaps they were a measure of Louis himself, independent of his teaching abilities. Yet, what he was doing in the classroom had not changed, and he had not changed either. On the other hand, the students were different. On average, the students in the private college had better standardized scores and came from a higher socioeconomic background, but was that enough to create such a dramatic shift in his evaluations? Were the evaluations just a measure of compatibility? If a good teacher could reach a certain group of students, and not another, did that then imply the evaluations were a measure of the students themselves, and only a secondary indicator of the instructor? Would not accepting his evaluations at face value suggest that "good" or "effective" teaching was whatever the students said it was? Nevertheless, shouldn't a teacher adapt to his or her students?

Louis, in an interview with his dean, suggested his classes were too rigorous for the students at his present school, but the dean assured him this was one of the primary reasons he was hired. "Our students need to be challenged," she said. Later, Louis smiled at the irony, mentally noting that the connection between rigor and learning had simply been assumed. No one had suggested his students be independently tested to discover if they were actually learning. Further, with her statement, the dean was admitting that she didn't believe the evaluations and learning were necessarily related. All Louis really knew was his students at the new school did not like him.

Introduction

There have been divisive issues among academicians in the past, but few have been as well researched and long-lasting as the discussion about the student evaluation of teaching (SET). Every aspect of the process has been investigated. Even the title of the evaluations became a matter of debate. The issue revolved around what students were doing, and what they were qualified to do, when they responded to the forms. Some suggested students were not qualified to evaluate instruction, but they could "rate" their experience in class by utilizing a ranking scale. In this view, the "evaluation" is not actually performed by students, but by professionals utilizing student input. Others insisted students were qualified to evaluate teaching because they are the ones actually present when the instruction takes place (Berk, 2013; Hativa, 2014). In this historical debate, it is enlightening to see what some of the oldest rating scales were called. Early instruments at the University of Washington were titled a "Survey of Student Opinion of Teaching" (Langen, 1966), while those at Michigan State were simply called the "Teacher Evaluation Sheet" (Dressel, 1961). At Purdue, it was a "Rating Scale for

Instruction" (Page, 1974) and at the University of Minnesota, the form was a "Student Opinion Survey" (Doyle, 1975). Note that the titles not only reflect a wide range of views, they also imply there was no consensus about what the process was designed to measure. Is the purpose to create a scale to supposedly measure a wide expanse, summarized by the word "instruction," or simply to survey "opinions?" Further, are the students attempting to measure an instructor, or what the instructor does? Consequently, for those who don't quibble about who is evaluating whom, the terms *Student Rating of Instruction* (SRI) or *Student Evaluation of Instruction* (SEI) are used, or the more common term, *Student Evaluation of Teaching* (SET) (see Baldwin, Ching, & Hsu, 2018). There are also a number of widely used evaluation instruments created by researchers and consultants, including the *Individual Development & Educational Assessment* (IDEA) created by a research and consulting group called IDEA out of Kansas State University, and a form created by Herbert Marsh called the *Student Evaluation of Educational Quality* (SEEQ). As can be seen from these titles, there is little agreement about what students are actually doing, and what is supposedly being measured.

In this book, we will simply refer to the process as the *Student Evaluation of Teaching* (SET), realizing, as we proceed, that the title may not reflect all the nuances of the research.

History

Even with a lack of consensus, and even while a vigorous debate was occurring questioning the validity of the process, the utilization of the evaluations became, for all practical purposes, universal. Initially, much of the research was positive and justified the popularity of the procedure. However, a dramatic increase in the utilization and impact of the evaluations occurred in the last several decades, ironically just as the research on SET was becoming increasingly negative.

Although investigations of SET date from the 1920s (Gump, 2007; Langen, 1966; Wachtel, 1998), one of the first more readily accessible research papers on SET was a report of a survey and subsequent development of an evaluation procedure at the University of Washington in 1944 (Guthrie, 1949). From that survey, procedures for faculty promotion and evaluation were developed. Some of the findings from the developmental process would sound familiar to someone studying the procedure almost 80 years later. No correlation was found between teaching effectiveness and research contribution, and full professors did not rate better than assistant professors. During the 1960s, there was an increase in the interest of students evaluating faculty, but many schools did not embrace SET, even though there was a growing consensus the instruments were, "systematic and tangible kinds of evidence for evaluation of teaching performance" (Centra, 1977, p. 19 of 26). By 1973, it was reported that 28% of campuses used some sort of student evaluation of instructors. By 1984, the number had increased to 68%, and by the early 1990s, 86% of universities used SET for important faculty decisions (Seldin, 1993). Business schools appear to be ahead of the curve; by 1994, about 95% of the deans of accredited business schools used the evaluations as a source of teaching information (Crumbley, 1995). Shortly thereafter, a study by the Carnegie Foundation found 98% of universities were using some form of student evaluations (Magner, 1997). At about the same time, another study reported 99% of business schools utilized evaluations by students, and deans placed a higher importance on these evaluations than either administrative or peer assessments (Comm & Manthaisel, 1998). A more recent American Association of University Professors (AAUP) poll (Vasey & Carroll, 2016) found only 4% of instructors reported the student evaluations were not required. Yet, even for this small group, the evaluations were still recommended. Currently, it would be difficult to find a university that does not utilize some form of the student evaluation of teaching.

Not only was the utilization of the instruments becoming normative, on many campuses SET became the most important and, in many cases, the only measure of teaching ability (Wilson, 1998). The instruments were also being used to make important non-instructional decisions. In one survey, almost 90% of accounting professors reported SET instruments were used to determine tenure decisions, and 70% said the evaluations were utilized to determine merit pay (Crumbley & Reichelt, 2009). Seldin (1999) reports a California dean as saying, "If I trust one source of data on teaching performance, I trust the students" (p. 15).

As would be expected, the universal utilization of an assessment that could establish reputations, merit pay, promotion, and tenure would be extensively researched. As early as 1990, it was reported at least 2,000 citations to SET existed (Feldman, 1997; Centra, 2003). One source stated there was close to 3,000 articles published on SET just in the 15 years between 1990 to 2005 (Al-Issa & Sulieman, 2007). Reports on the topic were so voluminous that many researchers began to utilize meta-analysis, in which a case was not a student or class average, but an entire published article (see Clayson, 2009; Cohen, 1980, 1981; Feldman, 1989; Spooren, Brockx, & Mortelmans, 2013; Stephen, Wright, & Jenkins-Guarnieri, 2011; Uttl, White, & Gonzalez, 2017 as examples). Nevertheless, little agreement had been made on key points. The defenders of the system were typically found in the colleges of education, and among those who consulted in the area. Some defended the evaluations almost as if they were religious tenets, and even referred to sources who identified contrary findings in strong and uncharacteristically negative terms (Aleamoni, 1999; Marsh, 1984; Marsh & Hattie, 2002; Marsh & Roche, 2000). These advocates typically had an advantage in the publication process since pedagogic research is the essential academic work of their profession. Other disciplines generally look upon research on instruction as less prestigious, and those opposed to the evaluation process are more dispersed among academic disciplines and more isolated in their publication outlets. They were, however, equally emphatic. In such an environment, it became relatively easy to select research findings that reinforced a point of view.

The following summary of the evaluation process is not free of these problems, but it does attempt to present information from a wider assortment of venues than is found in much of the traditional educational discipline outlets.

Question of Era

There are era and cultural matters related to SET. This is an issue which should influence our understanding of the evaluation process, but one that is rarely addressed. As previously indicated, there has been a change in the consensus about the validity of SET. Much of the current literature is negative, but, by the mid-1980s, the existing research on the evaluations was positive enough that negative attitudes toward them were referred to as "myths," "half-truths," and "witch hunts" (Aleamoni, 1987, 1999; Feldman, 1997; Marsh & Hattie, 2002; Theall & Franklin, 2001), a response that has been perpetuated by some compilers who have attempted to summarize the data (Gravestock & Gregor-Greenleaf, 2008; Hativa, 2014)

There were several reasons for this pre-millennial optimism.

First, a large amount of research had occurred. As a prominent scholar at the time noted, "Probably, students' evaluations of teaching effectiveness are the most thoroughly studied of all forms of personnel evaluation, and one of the best in terms of being supported by empirical research" (Marsh, 1987, p. 369). As previously noted, at least 2,000 reports of SET existed before 1990 (Feldman, 1997). Much of this research, especially the research published in the top journals, was positive.

Second, most of the research was conducted and published from within disciplines that had a philosophical and practitioner affinity toward the idea of student evaluation of instruction. Because of this orientation and the pioneering efforts of a relatively small group of noted researchers, studies into SET flowed almost exclusively out of a limited number of academic disciplines, which in time created what could be described as a self-perpetuating consensus. Although journals relating to educational issues existed in business and the physical sciences, references to them within mainline educational journals were largely missing from the SET literature. Several examples will serve. In Cashin's (1995) summary of SET findings, there are over 60 references, only one of which came from a source not associated with a college of education. Sixty-four percent of the authors are repeatedly cited. Feldman (1997) referenced over 150 sources in his excellent and carefully crafted article on identifying exemplary teachers. Only one of these is from a non-social science journal, and only five are from any source other than education and educational psychology. Marsh and Roche's (2000) research, published in the top journal of educational psychology, contains close to 60 references, none of which (other than statistical references) come from any discipline outside of education and psychology. In a summary article that has been widely cited, Marsh (2007) utilized extensive references. Not a single one came from the educational journals of STEM or business-related disciplines. While it would be expected the majority of research on SET would originate in education and educational psychology, and from a relatively small group of noted professionals,[1] it is the contention, and the experience, of this writer that outside research on SET was not generally considered for reference, or for publication, by researchers and editors within these discipline-specific areas. This began to change in the 1980s and expanded during the 90s, with a corresponding number of negative research findings being reported. As noted by Uttl, Cnudde, and White (2019), "authors from business and economics departments are now responsible for the substantial portion of newer, larger, and higher quality studies published in 1981 and after."

Third, cultures change and generations of students change as well. What students appreciate in an instructor in one generation might not be the same for students of another era. Although there is no known literature on the topic, it is likely these changes would affect the evaluations. Feldman (1987) conducted a meta-analysis that summarized the existing literature on research productivity's influence on SET. He found 33 published articles. The average date of publication for those sources was 1973. The students who gave their responses are now in their late 70s. When they were students, the average grade was a C and only 15% of the students received As. In addition, thinking of a student as a customer of an educational institution would not have been generally accepted. Currently, about 44% of American students get As and 70% have GPAs in the A to B range (Jaschik & Lerderman, 2016). Adjusted for population size, 2.3 times more people now go to college than in 1976,[2] and even adjusted for inflation, it now costs ten times more.[3] Many now simply assume students are consumers of education (Hativa, 2014).

It would be expected that modern students come from a wider cultural and social class background, and have different expectations about their educational experience, their relationship to instructors, and the educational institution than did students 30, 50, and even 70 years ago.

> The era and generational differences can be demonstrated with a personal note. When this writer was a sophomore in an engineering program, the best calculus lecturer was a man with strange mannerisms who chained-smoked through every lecture, literally lighting one cigarette from another and dropping the old one onto the floor. Before major exams, his classroom was standing-room only, jammed with students from other sections, because, it was believed, his students did better on the exams. At that time and at that school, one half or more of the entering students washed-out of the program and did not graduate. Compare this with the present, in which almost half of all students have an A average and schools are ranked not by the select few who graduate, but by the number of students retained.

Question of Motivation

An additional issue needs to be addressed before going further into the literature. Carlozzi (2018) recently noted,

> The literature on student evaluations of teaching (SETs) generally presents two opposing camps: those who believe in the validity and usefulness of SETs, and those who do not. Some researchers have suggested that "SET deniers" resist SETs because of their own poor SET results.
> (p. 359)

Indeed, critics could be accused of self-interest in finding fault with the SET process. Almost all university and college-level instructors believe themselves to be good teachers – it is the common conceit of the profession. An instrument that finds a person's self-concept to be incorrect is likely to be seen as wrong. On the other hand, if SET reaffirms a person's self-concept, it is likely to be assumed to be valid. This could result in biased perceptions of the SET process in which both detractors and advocates emotionally defend their position. It also creates the possibility of an ethical dilemma, whose resolution rests upon the validity of the instruments. If instructors with low evaluations demand to have these instruments removed from consideration for promotion, tenure, and merit pay, they could be seen as acting unethically *if* the instruments are valid. On the other hand, it would be unethical for instructors and administrators to advance SET *if* the instruments are invalid, and especially so if they individually benefited from their use.

The questions of motivation and ethics bring up another seldom-discussed issue. There is some evidence that preconceived attitudes and vested interests might bias research findings and interpretation. Carlozzi (2018) looked at 170 lead authors of published SET literature and compared their ratings on an online site, RateMyProfessors.com. It was found authors with higher evaluations had published research with more positive findings than did researchers with lower scores. In fact, authors with "negative attitudes" toward the evaluations were 14 times more likely to score below average on the evaluations than were lead authors with positive attitudes toward SET. In a recent meta-analysis, Uttl et al. (2019) looked at the foundational SET issue of learning and found researchers with a "vested interest" in finding a positive correlation between SET and learning generally found such correlations, while researchers with no vested interest in the evaluations found correlations between SET and learning to be "zero or nearly zero."

Nevertheless, to simply assume a critic of the SET process is someone who gets bad evaluations and a supporter is one who generally gets positive scores is an over simplification that ignores much of the history and research that will be reviewed in this book.

Intervening Variables

The underlying question that has motivated much of the research into the SET process has been: *What do the evaluations actually measure?* This has been approached, consistent with several different assumptions about the nature of instructional evaluation. Much of the research appears to assume the instruments are, at their core, measuring "good" or "effective" teaching, but may be contaminated by intervening variables (Centra & Gaubatz, 2000; Greenwald & Gillmore, 1997; Marsh, 1984; Rivera & Tilcsik, 2019). This approach looks for those aspects that might exist in the SET process and typically suggests ways "errors" can be corrected or minimized (see Sharon, 1970). The second approach assumes we do not know what SET is measuring, and the research attempts to clarify what that might be. A third approach generally ignores the core meaning of the evaluations, but centers on application, attempting to maximize the utilization of the instruments (see Berk, 2013; Linse, 2017). Most researchers appear to be unaware of this trichotomy, but tend to fall into one camp or another when interpreting the results of their findings.

Intervening variables, therefore, can be seen as aspects of the SET process which need to be controlled, or as evidence of what the instruments may or may not actually be measuring. It could be assumed, for example, that instructors of different genders should not receive significantly different evaluations. What explanation could be advanced that would suggest men make better teachers, on average, than women? If gender differences are found, does that imply that the instruments just need to be adjusted, or does it show that SET is invalid and does not measure "good" or "efficient" teaching? Or, in a purely utilitarian mode, do we really care as long as the procedure was carried out and no harm was allowed to occur to discriminated groups?

A number of intervening variables have been researched and debated, and are topically presented in the following chapters. After a review of these variables, a hypothesis that summarizes the SET process will be advanced.

Notes

1 Two excellent researchers who made significant contributions to the study of SET have been Herbert W. Marsh, professor emeritus at Oxford University, and Kenneth A. Feldman, formerly at Stony Brook University. All who defend the SET process make extensive reference to these two giants.
2 Statista, The Statistics Portal. Found at: www.statista.com/statistics/184272/educational-attainment-of-college-diploma-or-higher-by-gender.
3 IES, National Center for Education Statistics. Retrieved from https://nces.ed.gov/programs/digest/d07/tables/dt07_320.asp.

References

Aleamoni, L. M. (1987). Student rating myths versus research facts. *Journal of Personnel Evaluation in Education*, *1*(1), 111–119. https://doi.org/10.1007/BF00143282

Aleamoni, L. M. (1999). Student rating myths versus research facts from 1924 to 1998. *Journal of Personnel Evaluation in Education*, *13*(2), 153–166. https://doi.org/10.1023/A:1008168421283

Al-Issa, A., & Sulieman, H. (2007). Student evaluations of teaching: Perceptions and biasing factors. *Quality Assurance in Education*, *15*(3), 302–317. https://doi.org/10.1108/09684880710773183

Baldwin, S., Ching, Y., & Hsu, Y. (2018). Online course design in higher education: A review of national and statewide evaluation instruments. *TechTrends*, *62*, 46–57. https://doi.org/10.1007/s11528-017-0215-z

Berk, R. A. (2013). *Top 10 flashpoints in student ratings and the evaluation of teaching*. Sterling VA: Stylus.

Carlozzi, M. (2018). Rate my attitude: Research agendas and RateMyProfessor scores. *Assessment & Evaluation in Higher Education*, *43*(3), 359–368. https://doi.org/10.1080/02602938.2017.1348465

Cashin, W. E. (1995). *Student ratings of teaching: The research revisited* (IDEA Paper No. 32). Publication of the Center for Faculty Evaluation & Development, Division of continuing Education, Kansas State University. Retrieved from https://files.eric.ed.gov/fulltext/ED402338.pdf

Centra, J. A. (1977). *How universities evaluate faculty performance: A survey of department heads*. ERIC Document: ED 157445. https://eric.ed.gov/?id=ED 157445

Centra, J. A. (2003). Will teachers receive higher student evaluations by giving higher grades and less course work? *Research in Higher Education, 44*, 495–518. https://doi.org/10.1023/A:1025492407752

Centra, J. A., & Gaubatz, N. B. (2000). Is there gender bias in student evaluation of teaching? *The Journal of Higher Education, 71*(1), 17–33. https://doi.org/10.1080/00221546.2000.11780814

Clayson, D. E. (2009). Student evaluation of teaching: Are they related to what students learn? A meta-analysis and review of the literature. *Journal of Marketing Education, 31*(1), 16–30. https://doi.org/10.1177/0273475308324086

Cohen, P. A. (1980). Effectiveness of student-rating feedback for improving college instruction: A meta-analysis. *Research in Higher Education, 13*(4), 321–341. https://doi.org/10.1007/BF00976252

Cohen, P. A. (1981). Student ratings of instruction and student achievement: A meta-analysis of multi-section validity studies. *Review of Educational Research, 51*, 281–309. https://doi.org/10.3102/00346543051003281

Comm, C. L., & Manthaisel, D. F. X. (1998). Evaluating teaching effectiveness in America's business schools: Implications for service marketers. *Journal of Professional Service Marketing, 16*(2), 163–170. https://doi.org/10.1300/J090v16n02_09

Crumbley, D. L. (1995, Spring). On the dysfunctional atmosphere of higher education: Games professors play. *Accounting Perspectives, 1*, 67–77. Retrieved from https://oldrichkyn.com/DECAMEDU/Decline/stud_eval_n_lg.htm

Crumbley, D. L., & Reichelt, K. J. (2009). Teaching effectiveness, impression management, and dysfunctional behavior: Student evaluation of teaching control data. *Quality Assurance in Education, 17*(4), 377–392. https://doi.org/10.1108/09684880910992340

Doyle. K. O. (1975). *Student evaluation of instruction*. Lexington, MA: Lexington Books.

Dressel, P. L. (1961). *Evaluation in higher education*. Boston: Houghton Mifflin.

Feldman, K. A. (1987). Research productivity and scholarly accomplishment of college teachers as related to their instructional effectiveness: A review and exploration. *Research in Higher Education, 26*, 227–298. https://doi.org/10.1007/BF00992241

Feldman, K. A. (1989). The association between student ratings of specific instructional dimensions and student achievement: Refining and extending the synthesis of data from multisection validity studies. *Research in Higher Education, 30*, 583–645. https://doi.org/10.1007/BF00992392

Feldman, K. A. (1997). Identifying exemplary teachers and teaching: Evidence from student ratings. In R. P. Perry & J. C. Smart (Eds.), *Effective teaching in higher education: Research and practice* (pp. 368–395). New York: Agathon.

Gravestock, P., & Gregor-Greenleaf, E. (2008). *Student course evaluations: Research, models, and trends*. Toronto: Higher Education Quality Council of Ontario. https://doi=10.1.1.627.5590rep=rep1&type=pdf

Greenwald, A. G., & Gillmore, G. M. (1997). Grading leniency is a removable contaminant of student ratings. *American Psychologist*, *52*(11), 1209–1217. https://doi.org/10.1037/0003-066X.52.11.1209

Gump, S. E. (2007). Student evaluations of teaching effectiveness and the leniency hypothesis: A literature review. *Educational Research Quarterly*, *30*(3), 56–69. https://files.eric.ed.gov/fulltext/EJ787711.pdf

Guthrie, E. R. (1949). The evaluation of teaching. *Educational Record*, *30*, 109–115.

Hativa, N. (2014). *Student rating of instruction: Recognizing efective teacher* (2nd ed.). eBook: Oron Publications.

Jaschik, S., & Lederman, D. (2016). The 2016 inside higher ed survey of community college presidents. *Planning for Higher Education*, *45*(1), 127–142. Retrieved from https://search.proquest.com/openview/55902b3b7d84b8a561e377904c232a48/1?pqorigsite=gscholar&cbl=47536

Langen, T. D. F. (1966). Student assessment of teaching effectiveness. *Improving College and University Teaching*, *14*(1), 22–25. https://doi.org/10.1080/00193089.1966.10532490

Linse, A. R. (2017). Interpreting and using student ratings data: Guidance for faculty serving as administrators and on evaluation committees. *Studies in Educational Evaluation*, *54*, 94–106. https://doi.org/10.1016/j.stueduc.2016.12.004

Magner, D. K. (1997). Report says standards used to evaluate research should also be used for teaching and service. *The Chronicle of Higher Education*, *44*(2), A18–A19.

Marsh, H. W. (1984). Students' evaluation of university teaching: Dimensionality, reliability, validity, potential biases, and utility. *Journal of Educational Psychology*, *76*(5), 707–754. https://doi.org/10.1037/0022-0663.76.5.707

Marsh, H. W., & Hattie, J. (2002). The relation between research productivity and teaching effectiveness. *The Journal of higher Education*, *73*(5), 603–641. https://doi.org/10.1080/00221546.2002.11777170

Marsh, H. W., & Roche, L. A. (2000). Effects of grading leniency and low workload on students' evaluations of teaching: Popular myth, bias, validity, or innocent bystanders? *Journal of Educational Psychology*, *92*(1), 202–228. https://doi.org/10.1037/0022-0663.92.1.202

Marsh, W. H. (1987). Students' evaluations of university teaching: Research findings, methodological issues, and directions for future research. *International Journal of Educational Research*, *11*(3), 253–388. https://doi.org/10.1016/0883-0355(87)90001-2

Marsh, W. H. (2007). Do university teachers become more effective with experience? A multilevel growth model of students' evaluations of teaching over 13 years. *Journal of Educational Psychology*, *99*(4), 775–790. https://doi.org/10.1037/0022-0663.99.4.775

Page, C. F. (1974). *Student evaluation of teaching: The American experience*. London: Society for Research into Higher Education.

Rivera, L. A., & Tilcsik, A. (2019). Scaling down inequality: Rating scales, gender bias, and the architecture of evaluation. *American Sociological Review*, *84*(2), 248–274. https://doi.org/10.1177/0003122419833601

Seldin, P. (1993, July). The use and abuse of student ratings of professors. *Chronicles of Higher Education*, *21*, A40.

Seldin, P. (1999). *Changing practices in evaluation teaching: A practical guide to improving faculty performance and promotion/tenure decisions.* Bolton, MA. Anker Publishing Co., Inc.

Sharon, A. T. (1970). Eliminating bias from student ratings of college instructors. *Journal of Applied Psychology, 54*(3), 278–281. https://doi.org/10.1037/h0029241

Spooren, P., Brockx, B., & Mortelmans, D. (2013). On the validity of student evaluation of teaching: The state of the art. *Review of Educational Research, 83*(4), 598–642. https://doi.org/10.3102/0034654313496870

Stephen, L., Wright, S. L., & Jenkins-Guarnieri, M. A. (2011). Student evaluations of teaching: Combining the meta-analyses and demonstrating further evidence for effective use. *Assessment & Evaluation in Higher Education, 37*(6), 683–699. https://doi.org/10.1080/02602938.2011.563279

Theall, M., & Franklin, J. (2001). Looking for bias in all the wrong places: A search for truth or a witch hunt in student ratings of instruction? *New Directions for Institutional Research, 27*(5), 45–56. https://doi.org/10.1002/ir.3

Uttl, B., Cnudde, K., & White, C. A. (2019). Conflict of interest explains the size of student evaluation of teaching and learning correlations in multisection studies: A meta-analysis. *PeerJ, 7*, e7225. https://doi.org/10.7717/peerj.7225

Uttl, B., White, C. A., & Gonzalez, D. W. (2017). Meta-analysis of faculty's teaching effectiveness: Student evaluation of teaching ratings and student learning are not related. *Studies in Educational Evaluation, 54,* 22–42. https://doi.org/10.1016/j.stueduc.2016.08.007

Vasey, C., & Carroll, L. (2016, May–June). How do we evaluate teaching? *AAUP, reports & publications.* Retrieved from www.aaup.org/article/how-do-we-evaluate-teaching#.XrGdJm5FzIU

Wachtel, H. K. (1998). Student evaluations of college teaching effectiveness: A brief review. *Assessment & Evaluation in Higher Education, 23*(2), 191–211. https://doi.org/10.1080/0260293980230207

Wilson, R. (1998). New research casts doubt on value of student evaluations of professors. *The Chronicle of Higher Eduction, 44*(19), A12–A14. Retrieved from https://eric.ed.gove/?id=EJ558420

2 Potential Impacts of Gender Bias on Student Evaluations

Is There a Gender Bias in SET?

Nancy is an assistant professor looking for tenure. At her university, tenure is determined by a combination of factors including publications, research quality, service, reputation, and student evaluations. At the end of each year, she meets with her department chairperson. She is told she is doing well, but the administration has one concern. Her teaching evaluations are lower than what they would like. She is invited to sit in on classes taught by a tenured, male associate professor who gets excellent evaluations on a consistent basis. She does so, and incorporates much of what she is learning into her own classes, but at the end of the next year, her evaluations are still below average. Believing herself to be a good teacher, she complains to her chairperson that she is the victim of gender bias. Would the research confirm her assertion?

This is an important issue because as Lazos (2012) states, "anecdotally many women and minorities blame evaluations as a principle reason why they have not been able to get a foothold in academia" (p. 166). Are they correct?

Research on the question of whether gender creates differences in SET has provided mixed responses. Part of the confusion has resulted when intervening variables have not been clearly defined. There are a number of separate but interactive conditions that complicate the issue. These can be addressed by the following questions: 1) Do students evaluate instructors differently by the instructors' gender? In other words, is there a clear and widespread instructor gender bias? 2) Does the gender of the students influence evaluations, irrespective of the gender of instructors? Do students of one gender evaluate instruction differently than students from another? 3) Are potential gender main-effects generally small, but become significant when they interact with other variables?

Bias by Instructor's Gender

Early researchers, consistent with the times, assumed that if a gender bias existed, the bias would be against women. However, research during this period led investigators to state there was little or no gender-related effects in the evaluation process (Bennett, 1982; also see Feldman, 1993 for a review). One compiler even referred to gender influence on SET as one of several "myth(s)" about the evaluations (Aleamoni, 1987, 1999). However, these conclusions were not universally shared. Some argued gender bias was evident (Bernard, Kefauver, Elsworth, & Naylor, 1981), concluding that male instructors were evaluated more positively than female instructors.

Currently, several large non-experimental studies have shown little gender difference as a main effect (DeFrain, 2016; Rosen, 2018; Smith, Yoo, Farr, Salmon, & Miller, 2007). Yet, consistent with the differences in older studies, some credible research has found a systematic gender bias (Mengel, Sauermann, & Zölitz, 2017). The problem with a main-effect hypothesis is isolating the direct effect of gender on the evaluations. The lack of consensus could be interpreted as a result of historical and cultural gender bias interacting with other SET-related effects.

Bias by Students' Gender

Older studies found no influence of student gender on the evaluations (Page, 1974). Some reviewers, while generally agreeing with this conclusion, still admit there may be a difference in the way male and female students rate faculty (see Cashin, 1995). There is limited evidence male students give more negative evaluations than female students (Grayson, 2015; Mengel et al., 2017). It is not clear, however, whether these claims refer to main or interactive effects.

Interaction Bias Between Student and Instructor's Gender

Both historical and present research confirms an interactive gender bias in SET. Early studies showed both male and female students thought instructors of their own gender showed more "interest in students" (Elmore & LaPointe, 1975). Female students generally select women instructors as better teachers (Basow, 1998, 2000; Centra & Gaubatz, 2000), while male students give lower ratings to female instructors (Basow & Silberg, 1987; Mengel et al., 2017). Interestingly, there might not be a gender bias in selecting the "worst" instructors (Basow, 2000).

Bias Raised by Cultural or Societal Factors

While it would make a fascinating study in several academic disciplines, the writer knows of no direct test of the hypothesis that change in cultural gender perception is associated with change in SET. There is, however, considerable evidence that cultural attitudes are an important, if not primary, cause of gender bias in the SET process.

While Bennett (1982) suggested the literature base before the 1980s offered little evidence women received systematically lower marks than men, her results suggested female faculty members were nevertheless subject to culturally conditioned gender stereotypes. In fact, cultural gender role expectations have been consistently found in SET (Kaschak, 1981; Huebner & Magel, 2015; Miles & House, 2015). Female instructors, for example, are rewarded, relative to men, for being supportive and displaying "nurturing" behavior, and punished more for objective and authoritarian behavior (Langbein, 1994).

Culturally related biases can create some interesting interaction effects, which can be seen in students' reaction to academic rigor. Women are expected to be more nurturing and caring, while male instructors are associated more with higher standards – a finding which appears to have been consistent over long periods of time (Centra, 1972). It is not surprising then to find certain gendered differences. Female instructors are expected to be less demanding and give more As and Bs than male instructors (Huebner & Magel, 2015). Consistent with this, women get less of a boost in their evaluations for giving higher grades (Langbein, 1994) and, in male-dominated academic fields like engineering and business, female instructors are required to show higher standards than males (Basow & Silberg, 1987). However, in classes in which students don't expect rigor, female instructors are generally rated higher than male instructors (Foote, Harmon, & Mayo, 2003; Nargundkar & Shrikhande, 2014). Given these complexities, some researchers have concluded that female instructors must work harder to attain the same ratings given to men (Kierstead, D'Agostino, & Dill, 1988).

In addition to rigor, more recent studies indicate that students may have different learning expectations of instructors based on gender, *if* gender is combined with age. Older male instructors were perceived as encouraging learning by expecting good work and even by giving "too much work," while younger female instructors were considered more helpful, friendly, encouraging of questions, and having higher student rapport (Clayson, 2020; Wilson, Beyer, & Monteiro, 2014).

In summary, gender bias appears to be culturally related and is more subtle than assuming one gender will uniformly receive higher evaluations. Nevertheless, gendered expectations need not be equally applied. Some have concluded students have more "hostility" toward female instructors who violate expectations (Sprague & Massoni, 2005).

Reemergence of Bias

Perhaps because of cultural demands for more gender sensitivity, newer studies have increasingly found bias in SET, even in areas not expected to be related to gender (Boring, Ottoboni, & Stark, 2016; Clayson, 2019). Much of the newer information is coming from experimental studies in which instruction is held constant while students are led to believe it originated from teachers with different genders. At an American university, students were randomly assigned to one of four online discussion groups, each taught by one of two assistant instructors, one male and one female. Each instructor taught one group under their own identity and the second group under the other instructor's identity, so of the two groups who believed they had the female instructor, one actually had the male; and of the two groups who believed they had the male instructor, one actually had the female. At the end of the course, students rated their instructor through an online survey. The students rated the instructors they perceived to be female lower than those they perceived to be male, regardless of perceived teaching quality or actual gender of the instructor (MacNeil, Driscoll, & Hunt, 2015). A study of French students showed the same effect (Boring, 2017), as did another American study (Mitchell & Martin, 2018). In general, male students preferred male instructors, and the evaluations for both male and female instructors followed gender stereotypes, even when there was no difference between the students on standardized test results. In another study, Miles and House (2015) had students evaluate award-winning male and female professors. In all, they rated the male professors higher than the female professors. Moreover, the students attributed the male's excellent teaching to "academic qualities," while attributing the female's skill to "attractiveness."

Subtle hints of institutional gender bias can be found in how the SET instruments are structured. When the number of points in a scale are increased, say from a Likert scale of seven to a scale with ten positions, the top scales (in this case, nine and ten) are reserved for only those perceived as the very best, i.e., those in the top tenth or 20th percentile, while the top position in the Likert scale is more open to lower evaluations. It has been found that in male-dominated fields, male instructors will get higher evaluations than female instructors with ten-point scales than with six-point scales (Rivera & Tilcsik, 2019).

Language Bias

An intriguing method of studying bias is to compare the language used to describe individuals and events. Students have consistently been found to use different words to describe instructors based on gender (Mitchell & Martin, 2018), a phenomenon that has also been found in other cultures (Arceo-Gomez & Campos-Vazquez, 2019). A fascinating collection of data from RateMyPorfessors.com was assembled by Schmidt (2015), which showed an interesting pattern of anti-feminine bias. He looked at the frequency of words used in the written comments that accompany the numerical evaluations. Data selected from his large informational base were re-arranged by the present author and are presented in the table that follows. The table looks at the number of academic disciplines (majors), out of 25, in which a word or phrase was used more frequently for male or female instructors. As an example, the term "good teacher" is randomly distributed between male and female instructors, but the opposite term, "bad teacher," is found more frequently in female evaluations of 17 of 25 majors. The words "good," "funny," and "entertaining" are found in higher frequency in male evaluations in every major from which data was taken. The gender stereotype is reflected in the use of the word "nice," which was used in a higher frequency for females in all majors. In addition, the words "not recommended," "worst," "avoid," and "evil" are found in a higher frequency in female evaluations than male evaluations in almost all majors.

Table 2.1 Word Count Dominance by Majors
Word Frequency Dominance by Gender from 25 Academic Majors: Word Counts from Written Comments from RateMyProfessors.com (derived from Schmidt, 2015)

Word(s)	Male	Female	Ties	Sign Test
Learn	20	1	4[1]	<.001
Helpful	1	24	0	<.001
Good	25	0	0	<.001
Bad	6	13	6	<.001
Good teacher	7	5	13	.193
Bad teacher	4	17	4	.003
Work	0	25	0	<.001
Funny	25	0	0	<.001
Entertaining	25	0	0	<.001
Too hard	7	15	3	.041
Too hard (neg only)	13	9	3	.119
Nice	0	25	0	<.001
Worst	1	23	1	<.001
Evil	1	23	1	<.001
Death	4	16	5	.005
Avoid	4	21	0	<.001
Not recommended (For all reasons)	0	25	0	<.001
Not recommended (Neg only)	4	21	0	<.001

1 Of 25 different academic disciplines, the word "learn" had a higher frequency among male instructors in 20, a higher frequency for female instructors in only one major, and four showed no difference. This pattern resulting by chance has a probability less than 0.001.

Schmidt (2015) summarized his findings by judiciously stating students use a more "elaborate vocabulary" to criticize women who they believe to be unprofessional than when criticizing men.

A caveat is warranted here. Because a bias is shown to exist does not necessarily mean all aspects of the evaluation will be influenced by it. Nor does it offer proof the entire evaluation is biased by gender. Boring et al. (2016) claim the wrong questions have been asked. The issue, they state, is not whether men or women receive similar evaluations, but whether women would receive higher or lower scores for doing the same thing as men. Nevertheless, to the extent gender bias related to cultural stereotypes can influence SET independent of any change in the classroom challenges the validity of the SET process (Laube, Massoni, Sprague, & Ferber, 2007). According to the statistical discrimination theory (Phelps, 1972), evaluators will fall back on stereotypes to evaluate performance when unable to assess or process other relevant information, such as, in this case, actual teaching effectiveness (Boring, 2017).

Other Considerations

Gender bias, however, has professional, legal, and emotional consequences far beyond an investigation of the validity of an assessment instrument. Gender bias has been found to be stronger against female faculty who hold lower academic status (Carter, 2016). As a consequence, the SET process could hinder career opportunities. Mengel et al. (2017) summarized the problem: "The result that predominantly junior women are subject to the bias implies that two otherwise comparable female and male job candidates would go on the market with a significantly different teaching portfolio" (p. 27). Gender bias can also be seen in the students' reaction to ideas or social/political opinions which may be controversial. Utilizing an experimental design, Abel and Meltzer (2007) gave male and female students an identical written lecture about discrimination based on pay differences between men and women. Half thought the lecture came from a male and half thought it came from a female instructor. The male professor's lecture was rated more positively and as "less sexist" than the female professor's lecture. That is to say, the female professor was more negatively impacted for advancing a controversial issue than was the male professor. Both male and female students reacted the same. In another experimental study, an identical syllabus for a proposed psychology of human sexuality course, which was said to come from professors from a wide demographic, was given to students (Anderson & Kanner, 2011). Consistent with the previous study, "Lesbian and gay professors were rated as having a political agenda, compared to heterosexual professors with the same syllabus" (p. 1538).

Gender bias has another impact. Irrespective of other research findings, female instructors seem to be more emotionally impacted by the evaluations than males. Perhaps as a consequence, they are more likely to believe the evaluations are less valid and more harmful (Kogan, Schoenfeld-Tacher, & Hellyer, 2010).

Summary

1 Historically, research generally found few global differences (main effects) between the mean scores for male and female instructors. However, both historical and present data find numerous gender interaction effects in SET.
2 Gender roles are manifest in SET. Female instructors need to display more gender stereotypic behaviors than males for high evaluations.
3 Male instructors are expected to be more rigorous. There is some evidence to indicate that female instructors will receive higher evaluations in less rigorous classes.
4 Students use a different vocabulary when describing instructors of different genders.
5 If a male and a female instructor receive the same global evaluation, some of the reasons for that evaluation are likely to be different.
6 Overall, women are more negatively impacted by the SET process than are men.
7 Gender differences appear to be indications of social stereotypes and bias that may be found in students at any cultural period. Currently, consistent with the increased emphasize on gender issues, the research is finding more evidence for gender bias in SET. This suggests the pertinent research question might not be gender itself, but the effect of gendered cultural variables on the evaluations.

References

Abel, M. H., & Meltzer, A. L. (2007). Student ratings of a male and female professors' lecture on sex discrimination in the workforce. *Sex Roles*, *57*(3), 173–180. https://doi.org/10.1007/s11199-007-9245-x

Aleamoni, L. M. (1987). Student rating myths versus research facts. *Journal of Personnel Evaluation in Education*, *1*(1), 111–119. https://doi.org/10.1007/BF00143282

Aleamoni, L. M. (1999). Student rating myths versus research facts from 1924 to 1998. *Journal of Personnel Evaluation in Education*, *13*(2), 153–166. https://doi.org/10.1023/A:1008168421283

Anderson, K. J., & Kanner, M. (2011). Inventing a gay agenda: Students' perceptions of lesbian and gay professors. *Journal of Applied Social Psychology*, *41*(6), 1538–1564. https://doi.org/10.1111/j.1559-1816.2011.00757.x

Arceo-Gomez, E. O., & Campos-Vazquez, R. M. (2019). Gender stereotypes: The case of MisProfesores.com in Mexico. *Economics of Education Review, 72*, 55–65. https://doi.org/10.1016/j.econedurev.2019.05.007

Basow, S. A. (1998). Student evaluations: The role of gender bias and teaching roles. In L. H. Collins, J. C. Chrisler, & K. Quina (Eds.), *Career strategies for women in academe: Arming Athena* (pp. 135–156). Thousand Oaks, CA: Sage.

Basow, S. A. (2000). Best and worst professors: Gender patterns in students' choices. *Sex Roles, 43*(5/6), 407–417. https://doi.org/10.1023/A:1026655528055

Basow, S. A., & Silberg, N. T. (1987). Student evaluations of college professors: Are female and male professors rated differently? *Journal of Educational Psychology, 79*(3), 308–314. https://doi.org/10.1037/0022-0663.79.3.308

Bennett, S. K. (1982). Student perception of and expectation for male and female instructors: Evidence rating to the question of gender bias in teaching evaluations. *Journal of Educational Psychology, 74*(2), 170–170. https://doi.org/10.1037/0022-0663.74.2.170

Bernard, M. E., Kefauver, L. W., Elsworth, G., & Naylor, F. D. (1981). Sex-role behavior and gender in teacher-student evaluations. *Journal of Educational Psychology, 73*(5), 681–696. https://doi.org/10.1037/0022-0663.73.5.681

Boring, A. (2017). Gender biases in student evaluations of teaching. *Journal of Public Economics, 154*, 27–41. https://doi.org/10.1016/j.jpubeco.2016.11.006

Boring, A., Ottoboni, K., & Stark, P. B. (2016). Student evaluation of teaching (mostly) do not measure teaching effectiveness. *ScienceOpen.* https://doi.or/10.14293/S2199-1006.1.SOR-EDU.AETBZC.v1

Carter, R. E. (2016). Faculty scholarship has a profound positive association with student evaluations of teaching – Except when it doesn't. *Journal of Marketing Education, 38*(1), 18–36. https://doi.org/10.1177/0273475315604671

Cashin, W. E. (1995). *Student ratings of teaching: The research revisited* (IDEA Paper No. 32). Publication of the Center for Faculty Evaluation & Development, Division of continuing Education, Kansas State University. Retrieved from https://files.eric.ed.gov/fulltext/ED402338.pdf

Centra, J. A. (1972). *Two studies on the utility of student ratings for instructional improvement* (SIR Report No. 9). Princeton, NJ: Educational Testing Service.

Centra, J. A., & Gaubatz, N. B. (2000). Is there gender bias in student evaluation of teaching? *The Journal of Higher Education, 71*(1), 17–33. https://doi.org/10.1080/00221546.2000.11780814

Clayson, D. E. (2020). Student perception of instructors: The effect of age, gender, and political leaning. *Assessment & Evaluation in Higher Education, 45*(4), 607–616. https://doi.org/10.1080/02602938.2019.1679715

DeFrain, E. (2016). *An analysis of differences in noninstructional factors affecting teacher-course evaluations over time and across disciplines* (PhD Dissertation), The University of Arizona. Retrieved from https://repository.arizona.edu/bitstream/handle/ 10150/621018/azu_etd_14881_sip1_m.pdf?sequence=1

Elmore, P. B., & LaPointe, K. A. (1975). Effect of teacher sex, student sex, and teacher warmth on the evaluation of college instructors. *Journal of Educational Psychology, 67*(3), 368–374. https://doi.org/10.1037/h0076608

Feldman, K. A. (1993). College students' views of male and female college teachers: Part II Evidence from students' evaluations of their classroom teachers. *Research in Higher Education*, *34*(2), 151–211. https://doi.org/10.1007/BF00992161

Foote, D. A., Harmon, S. K., & Mayo, D. T. (2003). The impacts of instructional style and gender role attitude on students' evaluation of faculty. *Marketing Education Review*, *13*(2), 9–19. https://doi.org/10.1080/10528008.2003.11488824

Grayson, J. P. (2015). Repeated negative teaching evaluations: A form of habitual behavior? *Canadian Journal of Higher Education*, *45*(4), 298–321. https://files.eric.ed.gov/fulltext/EJ1086951.pdf

Huebner, L., & Magel, R. C. (2015). A gendered study of student ratings of instruction. *Open Journal of Statistics*, *5*(6), 552–567. https://doi.org/10.4236/ojs.2015.56058

Kaschak, E. (1981). Another look at sex bias in students' evaluations of professors: Do winners get the recognition that they have been given? *Psychology of Women Quarterly*, *5*(5), 767–772. https://doi.org/10.1177/036168438100505s12

Kierstead, D., D'Agostino, P., & Dill, H. (1988). Sex role stereotyping of college professors: Bias in students' rating of instructors. *Journal of Educational Psychology*, *80*(3), 342–344. https://doi.org/10.1037/0022-0663.80.3.342

Kogan, L. R., Schoenfeld-Tacher, R., & Hellyer, P. W. (2010). Student evaluations of teaching: Perceptions of faculty based on gender, position, and rank. *Teaching in Higher Education*, *15*(6), 623–636. https://doi.org/10.1080/13562517.2010.491911

Langbein, L. I. (1994, September). The validity of student evaluations of teaching. *PS: Political Science in Institutional Politics*, 545–552. https://doi.org/10.2307/420225

Laube, H., Massoni, K., Sprague, J., & Ferber, A. L. (2007). The impact of gender on the evaluation of teaching: What we know and what we can do. *NWSA Journal*, *19*(3), 87–104. www.jstor.org/stable/40071230

Lazos, S. R. (2012). Are students teaching evaluations holding back women and minorities? The perils of "Doing" gender and race in the classroom. In G. Gutierrez Muhs, Y. F. Niemann, C. G. Gonzalez, & A. P. Harris (Eds.), *Presumed incompetent: The intersections of race and class for women in academia*. Utah State University Press, University Press of Colorado. Retrieved from www.jstor.org/stable/j.ctt4cgr3k.19

MacNeil, L., Driscoll, A., & Hunt, A. N. (2015). What's in a name: Exposing gender bias in student rating of teaching. *Innovations in Higher Education*, *40*(4), 291–303. https://doi.org/10.1007/s10755-0149313-4

Mengel, F., Sauermann, J., & Zölitz, U. (2017). *Gender bias in teaching evaluations* (IZA Discussion Paper No. 11000). Retrieved from www.econstor.eu/bitstream/10419/170984/1/dp11000.pdf

Miles, P., & House, D. (2015). The tail wagging the dog; An overdue examination of student teaching evaluations. *International Journal of Higher Education*, *4*(2), 116–126. https://doi.org/10.5430/ijhe.v4n2p116

Mitchell, K. W., & Martin, J. (2018). Gender bias in student evaluations. *PS: Political Science & Politics*, *51*(2), 648–652. https://doi.org/10.1017/S10490965180001X

Nargundkar, S., & Shrikhande, M. (2014). Norming of student evaluations of instruction: Impact of noninstructional factors. *Decision Sciences Journal of Innovative Education, 12*(1), 55–72. https://doi.org/10.1111/dsji.12023

Page, C. F. (1974). *Student evaluation of teaching: The American experience.* London: Society for Research into Higher Education.

Phelps, E. S. (1972). The statistical theory of racism and sexism. *American Economic Review, 62*(4), 659–661. Retrieved from www.jstor.org/stable/1806107

Rivera, L. A., & Tilcsik, A. (2019). Scaling down inequality: Rating scales, gender bias, and the architecture of evaluation. *American Sociological Review, 84*(2), 248–274. https://doi.org/10.1177/0003122419833601

Rosen, A. S. (2018). Correlations, trends and potential biases among publicly accessible web-based student evaluations of teaching: A large-scale study of RateMyProfessors.com data. *Assessment & Evaluation in Higher Education, 43*(1), 31–44. https://doi.org/10.1080/02602938.2016.1276155

Schmidt, B. (2015, October 30). Rejecting the gender binary: A vector-space operation. *Ben's Bookworm Blog.* Retrieved from bookworm.benschmidt.org/posts/2015-10-30-rejecting-the-gender-binary.html.

Smith, S. W., Yoo, J. H., Farr, A. C., Salmon, C. T., & Miller, V. D. (2007). The influence of student sex and instructor sex on student ratings of instructors: Results from a college of communication. *Women's Studies in Communication, 30*(1), 64–77. https://doi.org/10.1080/07491409.2007.10162505

Sprague, J., & Massoni, K. (2005). Student evaluations and gendered expectations: What we can't count can hurt us. *Sex Roles, 53*(11/12), 779–799. https://doi.org/10.1007/s11199-005-8292-4

Wilson, J. H., Beyer, D., & Monteiro, H. (2014). Professor age affects student ratings: Halo effect for younger teachers. *College Teaching, 62*(1), 20–24. https://doi.org/10.1080/87567555.2013.825574

3 The Influence of Personality Traits on Student Evaluations

Do Personality Traits Influence the Evaluation Process?

Michael is a brilliant researcher and a good colleague, but most of his associates would classify him as being a bit "odd," or even "eccentric." He has little mannerisms that could appear to some as irritating. He would also be characterized as an introvert. He enjoys working alone and, even after years of teaching, he still gets nervous before almost every class. His shyness is interpreted by some students as a type of arrogance, or they believe he avoids interpersonal connections with his students because he does not care about them. Although students report that his classes are well organized, informative, and worthwhile, he still receives some of the lowest evaluations in his department. One of his friends claims that Michael is an excellent teacher, but his students just don't like him. Is that possible, and if so, is there anything Michael can do about it?

To the extent that personality is considered an intrinsic personal and long-lasting variable, its potential influence on the student evaluation of teaching can be both informative and troubling. Personality is determined in part by genetics (Gazzaniga & Heatherton, 2006). If personality traits are found to be highly related to SET, is it then possible to make long-term changes to achieve more positive evaluations? It is understandable, therefore, that defenders of the evaluation process would be sensitive to this issue.

Introduction

There is a scattered, but important literature base on the relationship between SET and personality. However, it does matter whose personality is being evaluated, and by whom (Poropat, 2014). The perceptions of the personality of others is generally related with SET, but self-evaluations are not. That is to say, instructors' perceptions of their own personality are not related to the evaluation given them by their students, nor, to a significant extent, are the perceptions of the students' own personality. However, the students' perception of their instructor's personality is strongly related to the evaluations, as are peer perceptions of an instructor (Renaud & Murray, 1996). It is of interest to realize that very little research has addressed this dichotomy, or speculated as to its cause.

Historical Development

In general, early researchers publishing from within education and educational psychology reported finding few personality traits that correlated with student ratings (Boice, 1992; Braskamp & Ory, 1994; Centra, 1993; Weaver, 1960). Yet, it was also reported that students form their opinions of a class and instructor very early in a course, and subsequent class and learning experiences did little to change that opinion (Ortinau & Bush, 1987; Sauber & Ludlow, 1988). Further, studies that manipulated classroom conditions found interesting experimental effects of instructors' personalities (Naftulin, Ware, & Donnelly, 1973; Widmeyer & Loy, 1988). One study by Harvard psychologists (Ambady & Rosenthal, 1993) investigated students' reactions to randomly selected 30-second clips of *soundless* videotapes of actual classroom instruction and found them highly correlated with end-of-course evaluations. Evaluations based on six-second exposures were no less significant than judgments based on 30-second clips. Personality traits identified by independent raters were highly correlated with the evaluations. In order, were *optimistic, confident, dominant, active, enthusiastic*, and *likable*. The raters' judgment of *professional* was not significantly correlated with the student evaluations.

These findings suggested a relationship between SET and personality, which was identified in other research. Feldman (1986) summarized the literature through the mid-1980s. He found that there was no evidence for a personality-evaluation association if personality was measured from the instructor's own perspective, but he did find the instructor's colleagues' perceptions were related to the evaluations. In addition, the students' perceptions of instructors were strongly related. The total associative measures of the students' perceptions, according to Feldman, range from 0.77 to 0.88, accounting for 60 to 75% of the variance. Evidence from other studies found a similar strong relationships (Erdle, Murray, & Rushton, 1985; Murray, Rushton, & Paunonen, 1990; Sherman & Blackburn, 1975; Marks, 2000). Feldman (1986) gave three interpretations for his findings. 1) The personality of an instructor is validly related to their teaching effectiveness. The instructor may show a different personality in class than in other environments, thus accounting for the lack of associations with the faculty member's own evaluations. 2) Both the measures of personality and teaching effectiveness are "contaminated" by other variables. For example, an instructor may be liked for any number of reasons, so students rate them as a good teacher and then state they have a pleasing personality. 3) The results of studies do say something valid about personality, but only within the students' perception. As an example, an instructor presents well-ordered lectures, which result in higher student achievement. Thus, the instructor gains a high evaluation and the students also "believe" the instructor is an organized person.

A study of business students resulted in an interesting path analysis (Clayson & Haley, 1990). Student perception of personality was found to be significantly related to every other factor in the study, including the students' perception of the instructor's knowledge and fairness and how much they thought they had learned. The research found the total effect of the perception on the student evaluation of faculty was very high, with each standard deviation change in personality resulting in a 0.83 standard deviation change in the evaluations.

Other evidence for a personality-evaluation association is more subtle. The evaluations have been found to be remarkably consistent for instructors, even over periods as long as 13 years (Marsh & Hocevar, 1991). Since most professionals are assumed to improve their performance with practice, what could the evaluations be measuring that would not change? Business students were asked, based on their own experience, what instructor traits would change over time. Instructional related attributes were seen as improving with experience, and students felt they would learn more from an instructor with these changes. They also felt experienced instructors would be fairer in testing and grading than less experienced professors. Instructor descriptions that contained words such as *responsive, interesting, cares, stimulating*, and *open* were selected as characteristics that the students had not seen as changing with more-experienced instructors. Since the mean scores of SET change very little over time, the students were essentially reinforcing the notion the evaluations are heavily biased toward personality variables and are less influenced by the instructor's perceived knowledge, fairness, or even the perception of student learning (Clayson, 1999).

In a more recent study of business students, Clayson and Sheffet (2006) compared measures of personality and evaluations at four different times during a term. They compared the *change* in the students' perception of their instructor's personality with the change in the evaluations over the last six weeks of the term. The personality-evaluation changes were highly related. In other words, even after the midterm, changes in evaluations (both positive and negative) for each instructor were highly related to changes in the students' perception of the instructor's personality. The study ruled out the possibility that the personality-evaluation association was a statistical artifact resulting from insufficient control of secondary variables.

To put these relationships into perspective, the data from Clayson and Sheffet's (2006) longitudinal study were entered into a cross-lagged model, which consisted of measurements made of the instructor's personality and the evaluation of teaching *before* the class began and at other times during the term. The model accounted for 66% of the total variance of personality at the end of the term and 70% of the total variance of the final evaluation. The pertinent aspect to this discussion is the association between personality measures and the evaluation. The model suggested that although personality and the evaluations are highly associated, the evaluation of an instructor is more predictive of subsequent measures of personality than personality is of predicting future evaluations. In other words, students appear to be making future judgments of an instructor's personality from their current impression of the instructor as a teacher, not the other way around. It is interesting to note, in light of future discussions of validity, that this model predicts the initial evaluations of the instructor made before any instruction, and even before the syllabus was distributed, it is significantly related to the final evaluations. This relationship was confirmed more directly in other analyses (Buchert, Laws, Epperson, & Bregman, 2008; Clayson, 2013).

The Assumption of Personality

Many educators simply assume, *a priori*, a relationship between effective teaching and personality-related characteristics. Lantos (1997) encourages instructors to use humor, "fun and games," learning students' names, and being "genuine" as methods of motivating students. Adrian, Phelps, and Totten (2017) suggested personal selling techniques used in business could be applied in a classroom setting, "to help faculty influence student evaluations in a way that is positive both for the faculty member and for the students" (p. 45). These assumptions have suggested to some that as higher education increasingly adopts a student satisfaction model, personality traits of instructors will become even more important (Gruber et al., 2012). After reviewing the literature and their own study, Foote, Harmon, and Mayo (2003) concluded, "those [instructors] who score highly on evaluations may do so not because they teach well, but simply because they get along well with students" (p. 17).

Other Personality Relationships

There is an interesting omission in this discussion. Is student personality related to the evaluations given to instructors? In other words, does a student with a certain personality structure tend to give higher or lower evaluations in general? Much of the published research on this topic is dated, and newer studies are almost nonexistent. However, as previously shown, self-perceptions, both of instructors and students, have been said to be unrelated to the evaluations. This appears to be counterintuitive. If an instructor's personality is related to the evaluations, as seen by students and peers, why is not the instructor's evaluation of self? In addition, why would a student high on a personality trait such as agreeableness not give a more agreeable evaluation? Further, it could be assumed that a trait like consciousness would be related to achievement, which, in turn, should be related to the evaluations. Nevertheless, some research found no "meaningful and consistent" relationship between the evaluations and student personality characteristics (Abrami, Perry, & Leventhal, 1982). However, other research has shown that such a relationship might exist. Page (1974) looked at nine studies conducted between 1965 and 1974. Six showed the evaluations and student personality characteristics were related, one indicated a possible connection, and two found no relationship at all. More recent research has found a weak connection between the Big-5 personality traits of students and the evaluations (Bonitz, 2011; McCann & Gardner, 2014; Patrick, 2011), specifically with the traits of agreeableness, openness, and consciousness. In addition, an interesting study out of Canada found the largest predictor of a third-year faculty evaluation was the student's evaluation in the first year (Grayson, 2015). That is to say, students who gave low (or high) evaluations tend to continue to give low (or high) evaluations irrespective of instructors or class topics. Tangential evidence from Australia found students rated their ideal instructor as having a personality similar to their own (Kim & MacCann, 2016).

Conclusion

In general, even though a research base exists, there has been a relative lack of interest in the implications of personality on SET. This is unfortunate for two reasons. First, some research has shown a personality-evaluation association of such magnitude that SET could be replaced with a personality inventory with little loss of predictive validity. Second, as will be demonstrated later, the perception of personality is a key element in determining what the evaluations are actually measuring.

Summary

1 The issue of personality as a factor in the outcome of the evaluations historically divided the defenders and the critics of the process.

Defenders suggest the effects of personality are small and, in general, those traits that do influence the evaluations can be modified, and/or are intrinsic to being a good teacher. Critics maintain the effect is large and personality traits that influence the outcome of the evaluations may be relatively permanent and ultimately not pertinent to what the evaluations should be measuring.

2 Studies have consistently found large and significant relationships between the students' perception of the personality of their instructors and SET. To a certain extent, personality seems to be the lens through which students look at other instructor variables when making their evaluations of instruction. In some studies, the impact of personality has been so strong that the SET instrument could be replaced with a personality inventory with little loss of predictive validity.

3 An instructor's assessment of their own personality seems to be largely unrelated to the evaluations given to them by their students. However, some evidence indicates there is a weak relationship between the students' own personality and SET.

4 One summarizing explanation would suggest that students judge a person as an instructor, and then assign personality traits consistent with that perception.

References

Abrami, P. C., Perry, R. P., & Leventhal, L. (1982). The relationship between student personality characteristics, teacher ratings, and student achievement. *Journal of Educational Psychology*, 74(1), 111–125. https://doi.org/10.1037/0022-0663.74.1.111

Adrian, C. M., Phelps, L. D., & Totten, J. W. (2017). Using personal selling techniques to influence student evaluation of faculty instruction. *Journal of Learning in Higher Education*, 13(2), 45–50. https://files.eric.ed.gov/fulltext/EJ1161828.pdf

Ambady, N., & Rosenthal, R. (1993). Half a minute: Predicting teacher evaluations from thin slices of nonverbal behavior and physical attractiveness. *Journal of Personality and Social Psychology*, 64, 431–441. https://doi.org/10.1037/0022-3514.64.3.431

Boice, R. (1992, Spring). Countering common misbeliefs about student evaluation of teaching. *ADE Bulletin*, 101, 2–8. Retrieved from https://podnetwork.org/content/uploads/V2-N2-Boice.pdf

Bonitz, V. S. (2011). Student evaluation of teaching: Individual differences and bias effects. *Graduate Theses and Dissertations*, 12211. Retrieved from https://lib.dr.iastate.edu/etd/12211

Braskamp, L. A., & Ory, J. C. (1994). *Assessing faculty work: Enhancing individual and institutional performances*. San Francisco: Jossey-Bass.

Buchert, S., Laws, E. L., Epperson, J. M., & Bregman, N. J. (2008). First impressions and professor reputation: Influence on student evaluations of instruction.

Social Psychology of Education, 11(4), 397–408. https://doi.org/10.1007/s11218-008-9055-1

Centra, J. A. (1993). Reflective faculty evaluations: Enhancing teaching and determining faculty effectiveness. San Francisco: Jossey-Bass.

Clayson, D. E. (1999). Students' evaluation of teaching effectiveness: Some implication of stability. Journal of Marketing Education, 21(1), 69–75. https://doi.org/10.1177/0273475399211009

Clayson, D. E. (2013). Initial impressions and the student evaluation of teaching. Journal of Education for Business, 88(1), 26–35. https://doi.org/10.1080/08832323.2011.633580

Clayson, D. E., & Haley, D. A. (1990, Fall). Student evaluations in marketing: What is actually being measured? Journal of Marketing Education, 12, 9–17. https://doi.org/10.1177/027347539001200302

Clayson, D. E., & Sheffet, M. J. (2006). Personality and the student evaluation of teaching. Journal of Marketing Education, 28(2), 149–160. https://doi.org/10.1177/0273475306288402

Erdle, S., Murray, H. G., & Rushton, J. P. (1985). Personality, classroom behavior and student ratings of college teaching effectiveness: A path analysis. Journal of Educational Psychology, 77(4), 394–407. https://doi.org/10.1037/0022-0663.77.4.394

Feldman, K. A. (1986). The perceived instructional effectiveness of college teachers as related to their personality and attitudinal characteristics. Research in Higher Education, 24(2), 139–213. https://doi.org/10.1007/BF00991885

Foote, D. A., Harmon, S. K., & Mayo, D. T. (2003). The impacts of instructional style and gender role attitude on students' evaluation of faculty. Marketing Education Review, 13(2), 9–19. https://doi.org/10.1080/10528008.2003.11488824

Gazzaniga, M. S., & Heatherton, T. F. (2006). Psychological science: Mind, brain, and behavior (2nd ed.). New York: W. W. Norton & Company.

Grayson, J. P. (2015). Repeated negative teaching evaluations: A form of habitual behavior? Canadian Journal of Higher Education, 45(4), 298–321. https://files.eric.ed.gov/fulltext/EJ1086951.pdf

Gruber, T., Lowrie, A., Brodowsky, G. H., Reppel, A. E., Voss, R., & Chowdhury, I. N. (2012). Investigating the influence of professor characteristics on student satisfaction and dissatisfaction: A comparative study. Journal of Marketing Education, 34(2), 165–178. https://doi.org/10.1177/0273475312450385

Kim, L. E., & MacCann, C. (2016). What is students' ideal university instructor personality? An investigation of absolute and relative personality preferences. Personality and Individual Differences, 102, 190–203. https://doi.org/10.1016/j.paid.2016.06.068

Lantos, G. P. (1997). Motivating students: The attitude of the professor. Marketing Education Review, 7(2), 27–38. https://doi.org/10.1080/10528008.1997.11488588

Marks, R. B. (2000). Determinants of student evaluations of global measures of instructor and course value. Journal of Marketing Education, 22(2), 108–119. https://doi.org/10.1177/0273475300222005

Marsh, H. W., & Hocevar, D. (1991). Students' evaluation of teaching effectiveness: The stability of mean rating of the same teachers over a 13-year period. *Teaching & Teaching Education, 7*(4), 303–314. https://doi.org/10.1016/0742-051X(91)90001-6

McCann, S., & Gardner, C. (2014). Student personality differences are related to their responses on instructor evaluation forms. *Assessment & Evaluation in Higher Education, 39*(4), 412–426. https://doi.org/10.1080/02602938.2013.845647

Murray, H. G., Rushton, J. P., & Paunonen, S. V. (1990). Teacher personality traits and student instructional ratings in six types of university courses. *Journal of Educational Psychology, 82*(2), 250–261. https://doi.org/10.1037/0022-0663.82.2.250

Naftulin, D. H., Ware, J. E., & Donnelly, F. A. (1973). The doctor fox lecture: A paradigm of educational seduction. *Journal of Medical Education, 48*, 630–635. Retrieved from https://adrianmarriott.net/logosroot/papers/DrFoxSpoof.pdf

Ortinau, D. J., & Bush, R. P. (1987, Spring). The propensity of college students to modify course expectations and its impact on course performance information. *Journal of Marketing Education, 9*, 42–52. https://doi.org/10.1177/027347538700900108

Page, C. F. (1974). *Student evaluation of teaching: The American experience*. London: Society for Research into Higher Education.

Patrick, C. L. (2011). Student evaluations of teaching: Effects of the big five personality traits, grades and the validity hypothesis. *Assessment & Evaluation in Higher Education, 36*(2), 239–249. https://doi.org/10.1080/02602930903308258

Poropat, A. E. (2014). Other-rated personality and academic performance: Evidence and implications. *Learning and Individual Differences, 34*, 24–32. https://doi.org/10.1016/j.lindif.2014.05.013

Renaud, R. D., & Murray, H. G. (1996). Aging, personality, and teaching effectiveness in academic psychologists. *Research in Higher Education, 37*(3), 323–340. https://doi.org/10.1007/BF01730120

Sauber, M. H., & Ludlow, R. R. (1988). Student evaluation stability in marketing: The importance of early class meetings. *The Journal of Midwest Marketing, 3*, 41–49.

Sherman, B. R., & Blackburn, R. T. (1975). Personal characteristics and teaching effectiveness of college faculty. *Journal of Educational Psychology, 67*(1), 124–131. https://doi.org/10.1037/h0078680

Weaver, C. H. (1960). Instructor rating by college students. *Journal of Educational Psychology, 51*(1), 21–25. https://doi.org/10.1037/h0047109

Widmeyer, W. N., & Loy, J. M. (1988). When you're hot, you're hot! warm-cold effects in first impressions of persons and teaching effectiveness. *Journal of Educational Psychology, 80*, 118–121. https://doi.org/10.1037/0022-0663.80.1.118

4 Halo Effects Impacting on Student Evaluations

Do Aspects of the Instructional Environment, Unrelated to the Purposes of Instruction, Influence the Evaluations?

> Bill is reaching retirement age. He has been teaching for almost 40 years and has consistently received average evaluations. Even though he has taught a variety of topics to different generations of students, his evaluations have remained essentially unchanged. He realized he is not very dramatic in his teaching style, and even though he had never given it much thought, with the advent of social media and ubiquitous smartphones, he has come to realize he is not as "current" and "attractive" as many of his colleagues. After reading a popular book about the effects of physical attractiveness and age on social interactions, he began to wonder if his student evaluations might not be influenced by his physical appearance, which, he assumes, he can do little to change.

What do we tell Bill? Is it possible SET is modified by factors that would not normally be considered relevant to "effective" or "good" teaching? If two instructors taught the same material in an identical fashion, would the taller or more attractive instructor receive a better evaluation? Over a hundred years ago, Edward Thorndike (1920) wrote:

> In a study made in 1915 of employees of two large industrial corporations, it appeared that the estimates of the same man in a number of different traits such as intelligence, industry, technical skill, reliability, etc., etc., were very highly correlated and very evenly correlated. It consequently appeared probable that those giving the ratings were unable to analyze out these different aspects of the person's nature and achievement and rate each in independence of the others. Their ratings were apparently affected by a marked tendency to think of the person in general as rather good or rather inferior and to color the judgments of the qualities by this general feeling. This same constant error

toward suffusing ratings of special features with a halo belonging to the individual as a whole appeared in the ratings of officers made by their superiors in the army.

(p. 25)

The Halo Effect, as seen by Thorndike, occurs when some aspect of a person or thing over-shadows or influences other unrelated attributes being judged or measured. An often-used example is physical attractiveness. In its simplest form: *Attractive is good, therefore attractive persons are good. Therefore, what these good persons do is good.* To the extent halo effects are present in the evaluations, it would be expected that perceived aspects of the instructor will be associated with the evaluation ratings, even if those perceptions are not generally considered to be relevant to what SET is supposedly trying to measure. It is difficult, for example, to create a hypothesis that would allow more attractive individuals, or taller persons, to be more "effective" as an instructor. Nevertheless, there is evidence that even brief exposures to personal characteristics create halos which can have long-lasting effects on SET. Ambady and Rosenthal (1993) investigated the effects of short videos of non-verbal behavior on future evaluations. They reported,

> results were striking. First, we found that the ratings of complete strangers based on very thin slices of teachers' nonverbal behavior (video clips from 2 s to 10 s long) predicted with surprising accuracy the ratings of the same teachers by people who had substantial interactions with those teachers (students and supervisors, for example). Moreover, judgments based on 30-s exposures (three 10-s clips of each teacher) were not significantly more accurate than judgments based on 6-s exposures (three 2-s clips of each teacher).

(p. 438)

Their findings were replicated by a more recent study (Tom, Tong, & Hesse, 2010).

The possible consequences of a halo effect were put into perspective by Keeley, English, Irons, and Henslee (2013), "Uniformly high ratings may not correspond to uniformly excellent teaching behaviors, and one area of poor performance might drag all others if students find it particularly salient" (p. 455).

Physical Attractiveness

Do Physically Attractive Instructors Get Higher Evaluations?

Contrary to some research, the answer to the question appears to be yes. However, the question needs to be modified. Under identical classroom and instructional conditions, would a more physically attractive instructor get higher evaluations? Naturalistic research utilizing the online evaluation platform RateMyProfessors has shown a very strong associational effect between the evaluations and physical attractiveness (Carter, 2016; Freng & Webber, 2009; Riniolo, Johnson, & Sherman, 2006). Instructors judged by students to be "hot" received significantly higher evaluations, even when controlled by academic discipline and gender. Unfortunately, the variable of interest in these studies is undefined. Students can select an instructor as being "hot" for a variety of reasons. We could assume that, generally, the selection would be based on physical attractiveness, but students may see an instructor as "hot" because of the instructor's personality, or any number of other causes. The measure is, however, interesting in that the students are signaling that they do have a bias by utilizing this particular response option.

In an experiment conducted over 40 years ago, nine- and 13-year-old students watched a videotaped class taught by a female teacher. It was found that when a teacher appeared attractive, she was rated as more competent and better able to stimulate and motivate students than when she looked unattractive (Chaikin, Gillen, Derlega, Heinen, & Wilson, 1978). These students were not college aged, but consistent with findings already discussed, no effects on actual academic performances were found due to the teacher's nonverbal characteristics. More recent studies have shown an attractiveness halo (Feeley, 2002). Gurung and Vespia (2007) found attractiveness was significantly correlated with student ratings of learning, grades, and professors being more approachable, likeable, and enjoyable. Attractiveness was even associated with attendance, but not to "class difficulty." Hamermesh and Parker (2005) looked at six independent measures of attractiveness and compared these with evaluation ratings. They state, "The estimates leave little doubt that measures of perceived beauty have a substantial independent positive impact on instructional ratings by undergraduate students" (p. 374). The impact of attractiveness was found within university departments and even within particular courses. The biasing effect of physical attractiveness appears to be stronger when "explicit information" about the subject is absent (Jackson, Hunter, & Hodge, 1995).

Hamermesh and Parker (2005) warn that the physical attractiveness effect could be the result of bias or actual productivity, and it may be impossible to determine which. In fact, a case has been made that the consequences of attractiveness may be based on actual performance. Kanazawa and Kovarb (2004) argued that if several assumptions were true, beautiful people are likely to be more intelligent and may therefore be more productive. If we assume intelligence and beauty both have large heritable components, and more intelligent people are more likely to attain a higher status, then that status might allow them to find more attractive mates, and therefore attractiveness and achievement become linked. However, a meta-analysis of the existing literature before 1995 found no association between attractiveness and competence (Jackson et al., 1995). Nevertheless, and for whatever reason, physical appearance does appear to influence the evaluations (Wright, 2000).

The Dr. Fox Effect

Do Charisma and Personal Mannerisms Change the Evaluations?

The Dr. Fox experiment was conducted in 1970 at the University of Southern California School of Medicine (Naftulin, Ware, & Donnelly, 1973). Subjects consisted of 55 professionals: two small groups of psychiatrists, psychologists and social work educators, and a third group of "educators and administrators." A professional actor, given the name of Dr. Myron L. Fox, presented a lecture on mathematical game theory, a topic unfamiliar to the subjects. He was coached to use "double talk, neologisms, non sequiturs, and contrary statements" interspersed with humor and "meaningless references to unrelated topics," but to do so in a dramatic and charismatic fashion. The hypothesis of the study was defined as: "Given a sufficiently impressive lecture paradigm, an experienced group of educators participating in a new learning situation can feel satisfied they have learned despite irrelevant, conflicting, and meaningless content conveyed by the lecturer" (p. 632). Even though the presentation was nonsense, 76% of the professionals said the material was well-organized, 85% said the speaker used enough examples to clarify his material, and 91% indicated he stimulated their thinking. Ironically, the study never attempted to measure perceived learning, a point made by the study's critics (see Marsh & Ware, 1982). All of the questions asked could be answered in the positive by someone who thought they learned nothing.

The idea that professionals could be fooled into confusing unrelated style with content understandably created a number of responses in the SET literature, much of it attacking the concept. A leading example was a careful review by Marsh and Ware (1982).

> This study [the Dr. Fox study] was fraught with methodological weaknesses, including lack of an adequate control group, a poor rating instrument, problems of generalizability to college classrooms, and so on.... Nevertheless, many critics of instructional evaluation have cited the study as evidence of the invalidity of student ratings.
>
> (p. 126)

Marsh and Ware went on to find no support for the Dr. Fox Effect, except for an interesting caveat. When students were not given an incentive to learn, the effect of instructor expressiveness on the evaluations had a greater impact on the results, essentially supporting the Dr. Fox Effect. Nevertheless, this study was interpreted as evidence against the idea. Almost 20 years later, Theall and Franklin (2001) included the Dr. Fox Effect as one of the elements of a "witch hunt" to discredit SET.

Nevertheless, evidence for the Dr. Fox Effect continued to appear (Ware & Williams, 1979, 1980). Murray (1983) conducted an interesting study in which 54 full-time instructors in the social sciences were separated into three group (low, medium, high) based on their evaluation scores over a period of four years. A group of 49 trained students visited each class for a total of 18 to 24 hours and recorded their observations on a 60-item inventory. The student raters did not know which group their evaluated instructor was in, and the instructors did not know how they were being evaluated. It was found that instructors who showed "facial expressions," "energy and excitement," and "moves about while lecturing" had received higher evaluations by their students. It was also found that instructors who spoke more rapidly and more "expressively and emphatically" had been rated higher. In addition, a factor analysis of the 60 items found "enthusiasm" was the second-strongest factor in the study (out of nine) and it accounted for over 12% of the difference variance of the study. In a study of UK students, charismatic factors were found to account for 67% of the variation in instructors' lecture ability, as seen by students (Shevlin, Banyard, Davies, & Griffiths, 2000). The authors concluded, "The SET ratings were demonstrated to be significantly affected by the students' perception of the lecturer on a variable that should be unrelated to assessments of teaching ability, thereby questioning the validity of this particular scale" (p. 402).

More recent findings have consistently found the Dr. Fox Effect, especially with the influence of instructor fluency (Carpenter, Mickes, Rahman, & Fernandez, 2016), but with cautionary restrictions. Carpenter, Wilford, Kornell, and Mullaney (2013) conducted two experiments:

> In both experiments, the fluent instructor was rated significantly higher than the disfluent instructor on traditional instructor evaluation questions, such as preparedness and effectiveness. However, in both experiments, lecture fluency did not significantly affect the amount of information learned. Thus, students' perceptions of their own learning and an instructor's effectiveness appear to be based on lecture fluency and not on actual learning.
>
> (p. 1350)

Another study (Peer & Babad, 2014) found:

> The Dr. Fox effect was indeed consistently replicated in all samples. However, the originally proposed notion of educational seduction leading to presumable (illusory) student learning was ruled out by the empirical findings: Students indeed enjoyed the entertaining lecture, but they had not been seduced into believing they had learned.
>
> (p. 36)

However, the implications assumed by the learning interaction have a flaw. As will be shown in a subsequent chapter, there is little evidence for a relationship between SET and actual learning, and students many times avoid and dislike factors which lead to learning (Appleton-Knapp & Krentler, 2006). An example can be shown with attendance policies. Students admit the policies helped them to attend class, and they acknowledged coming to class would help them get better grades, but they still expressed a dislike of attendance policies (Verbeeten & van Hoof, 2007). Students appear to want Dr. Fox even if they do not learn as much, and seem willing to reward him on the evaluations. Those outside of education do not find this unusual. An article in *The Atlantic* (Lahey, 2016) summarized this by stating, "Education, at its most engaging, is performance art." As a SET critic, Paul Trout (1997) put it,

> To improve your evaluation scores, you are going to have to accept the fact that college "teaching" has less to do with knowledge and information and more with convincing students you are one hell of a lecturer, even when spouting nonsense. It's not what you communicate, but *how*.

Political Leanings

Does Political Orientation Influence SET?

Given the political controversies that have been found among students from the 1960s onward, and the importance some educational professionals place on political movements, it comes as a surprise to find the issue to be almost entirely missing in studies of SET. Reviews of the literature never mention a political bias (see Benton & Cashin, 2014; Wachtel, 1998). Given SET instruments do not attempt to measure political leanings of either the instructor or the student, and the finding that students tend to give higher evaluations to instructors who appear to be willing to discuss different points of view (Dixon & McCabe, 2006), it may be understandable that this issue has been overlooked. Nevertheless, there are some cogent arguments which would suggest such a relationship ought to exist (see Kelly-Woessner & Woessner, 2006).

A limited number of studies are available, all from political science, and all from the same research team. Even though most instructors attempt to remain politically neutral in the classroom, students seem able to identify the political leanings of their professors (Kelly-Woessner & Woessner, 2008). In general, students in political science classes associated caring and encouragement with a more liberal instructor, but more strongly rewarded instructors whose political views matched their own. All the overall assessment measures in one study were significantly associated with partisan differences (Kelly-Woessner & Woessner, 2006). Further, it was found that students who believe their instructor shared their political beliefs reported "more learning, higher levels of effort, and greater interest in the subject" than students who perceived their professor to be a "political foe" (Kelly-Woessner & Woessner, 2008).

In other words, students gave higher evaluations to instructors who they believed held the same political orientation as themselves. Whether this pattern exists with students who are not interested in the study of politics remains to be seen.

Instructor's Age and Experience

Does the Instructor's Age Matter to Students?

The definitive research on the effects of age on SET was conducted by Feldman (1983), who performed a meta-analysis which included published research extending into the late 1970s. Between 1936 through 1977, he found no studies showing that instructors got higher evaluations as they got older (six showed no correlation with age, and six showed a negative correlation). Between 1965 through 1979, he found two that showed a positive association between SET and experience, eight that showed no relationship, and five studies with a negative relationship. Cashin (1995) summarized Feldman's findings by saying that, in general, years of teaching was not correlated with SET, and if an association was found, it tended to be negative, a finding further reinforced by other sources (Braskamp & Ory, 1994; Yermack & Forsyth, 2016).

One of the oldest accessible studies of the evaluation procedure (Guthrie, 1949) found no important differences between the ratings of instructors by academic ranks. This finding was reinforced by professors' perceptions. When instructors were asked to identify characteristics of "effective" teachers, they found age and length of teaching to be unrelated to being "effective" (Wilson, Dienst, & Watson, 1973). In other words, on average, years of experience did not change SET. Using longitudinal measures, social science instructors showed high consistency in SET scores over a four-year period (Murray, 1983), and later research found the evaluations were consistent over periods as long as 13 years. Prior experience did not modify this consistency (Marsh & Hocevar, 1991). Even more recent research has indicated that, in some settings, new instructors actually get better evaluations than do older, experienced instructors (Carrell & West, 2010). There does appear to be a popularity bias favoring younger instructors (McPherson, Jewell, & Kim, 2009).

The literature seems to be suggesting that if the instruments are valid, experience does not improve performance. Since SET is almost universal, we could also conclude that years of evaluations do not improve instruction. These findings present us with a conundrum. While they may be interpreted as showing a structural consistency that could be seen as a sign of reliability, they also indicate a logical inconsistency. In what professional activity does years of practice not improve performance? If the evaluations are valid measures of "effective" and/or "good" teaching, then years of experience do not improve an instructor's ability to provide these to his or her students. If anything, the instructor's ability decreases with practice (Renaud & Murray, 1996). An interesting alternative hypothesis was proposed by Wilson, Beyer, and Monteiro (2014). They suggest that any improvement, which may be found in the evaluations by experience, is being canceled by the students' age bias.

One recent study attempted to combine these elements (Clayson, 2020). Students were asked to rank instructors based on eight combinations of gender, age, and political orientation. No other information was given about the instructors. For example, an instructor could be identified as a male, older, and conservative (MOC), or as a female, young, and liberal (FYL). A ranking was done for both business and humanity classes, both in terms of how much the student would learn and how helpful the instructor would be. The students, 287 in total, with half female and evenly distributed between business and liberal arts students, ranked the instructors. Students believed they would learn the most in a business class from a male, older conservative, and in a humanity class from a male, older liberal. However, they believed a male, younger conservative would be the most helpful in business, while a female, young liberal would be the most helpful in a humanity class. In general, students believed they would learn the most from older, male instructors, but would find instructors who are helpful to be younger and to differ by gender and political orientation. This perception of students was also found by Wilson et al. (2014), who reported older males were seen by students as expecting good work, and, if anything, gave too much work, while younger females were seen as encouraging questions and creating rapport with students. In Clayson's study, political orientation was important in humanity classes, but not in business classes. Both female and male students, and both business and non-business students, indicated no significant differences in instructor rankings by gender or by age standing alone. Even with its limited size and restricted sample, the study demonstrated students do have age, gender, and political stereotypes when thinking about their instructors. The study also showed an interesting difference in the way students perceive instructors who could potentially encourage learning compared with those who were being helpful. They separated the two.

Feeling Good

Something as simple as having a tasty treat can sometimes modify SET. Students in three classes taught by the same instructor attended discussion sections taught by a teaching assistant. The faculty instructor was evaluated by the students in the discussion classroom rather than in class. Half of the students received chocolates prior to filling out the evaluation and half did not. The SET administrator emphasized that he was the source of the chocolate, *not* the instructor. Eight of nine scales about the instructor were found to be higher in the chocolate group compared to the control group. The chocolate group stated the class was more intellectually challenging, students were encouraged to participate more in class, the class was better compared to other classes, and the instructor was friendlier toward students than the ratings made by the control group (Youmans & Jee, 2010). Evidently, even with medical students, chocolate cookies have similar effects (Hessler et al., 2018).

Summary

1   Halo effects exist in SET.
2   Characteristics of the instructor, such as gender, physical attractiveness, fluency, and age influence the evaluations, even when those characteristics appear unrelated to effective or good instruction.
3   Halo effects do not appear to influence objective student learning. Some researchers hypothesize halo effects are therefore irrelevant to the evaluation process, while an alternative hypothesis would state they constitute a summary of what SET actually measures.

References

Ambady, N., & Rosenthal, R. (1993). Half a minute: Predicting teacher evaluations from thin slices of nonverbal behavior and physical attractiveness.

Journal of Personality and Social Psychology, 64, 431–441. https://doi.org/10.1037/0022-3514.64.3.431

Appleton-Knapp, S. L., & Krentler, K. A. (2006). Measuring student expectations and their effects on satisfaction: The importance of managing student expectations. *Journal of Marketing Education, 28*(3), 254–264. https://doi.org/10.1177/0273475306293359

Benton, S. L., & Cashin, W. E. (2014). *Student ratings of teaching: A summary of research and literature* (IDEA PAPER No. 50). Manhattan, KS: The IDEA Center. Retrieved from http://citeseerx.ist.psu.edu/viewdoc/download?doi=10.1.1.388.8561&rep=rep1&type=pdf

Braskamp, L. A., & Ory, J. C. (1994). *Assessing faculty work: Enhancing individual and institutional performances*. San Francisco: Jossey-Bass.

Carpenter, S. K., Mickes, L., Rahman, S., & Fernandez, C. (2016). The effect of instructor fluency on students' perceptions of instructors, confidence in learning, and actual learning. *Journal of Experimental Psychology Applied, 22*(2), 161–172. https://doi.org/10.1037/xap0000077

Carpenter, S. K., Wilford, M. M., Kornell, N., & Mullaney, K. M. (2013). Appearances can be deceiving: Instructor fluency increases perceptions of learning without increasing actual learning. *Psychonomic Bulletin & Review, 20*(6), 1350–1356. https://doi.org/10.3758/s13423-013-0442-z

Carrell, S. E., & West, J. E. (2010). Does professor quality matter? Evidence from random assignment of students to professors. *Journal of Political Economy, 118*(3), 409–432. https://doi.org/10.1086/653808

Carter, R. E. (2016). Faculty scholarship has a profound positive association with student evaluations of teaching – Except when it doesn't. *Journal of Marketing Education, 38*(1), 18–36. https://doi.org/10.1177/0273475315604671

Cashin, W. E. (1995). *Student ratings of teaching: The research revisited* (IDEA Paper No. 32). Publication of the Center for Faculty Evaluation & Development, Division of continuing Education, Kansas State University. Retrieved from https://files.eric.ed.gov/fulltext/ED402338.pdf

Chaikin, A. L., Gillen, B., Derlega, V. J., Heinen, J. R., & Wilson, M. (1978). Students' reactions to teachers' physical attractiveness and nonverbal behavior: Two exploratory studies. *Psychology in the Schools, 15*(4), 588–595.

Clayson, D. E. (2020). Student perception of instructors: The effect of age, gender, and political leaning. *Assessment & Evaluation in Higher Education, 45*(4), 607–616. https://doi.org/10.1080/02602938.2019.1679715

Dixon, J., & McCabe, J. (2006). Competing perspectives in the classroom: The effect of sociology students' perceptions of 'balance' on evaluations. *Teaching Sociology, 34*(2), 111–125. https://doi.org/10.1177/0092055X0603400202

Feeley, T. H. (2002). Evidence of halo effects in student evaluations of communication instruction. *Communication Education, 51*(3), 225–236. https://doi.org/10.1080/03634520216519

Feldman, K. A. (1983). The seniority and instructional experience of college teachers as related to the evaluations they receive from their students. *Research in Higher Education, 5*, 243–288. https://doi.org/10.1007/BF00992080

Freng, S., & Webber, D. (2009). Turning up the heat on online teaching evaluations: Does "Hotness" matter? *Teaching in Psychology, 36*(3), 189–193. https://doi.org/10.1080/00986280902959739

Gurung, R. A. R., & Vespia, K. (2007). Looking good, teaching well? Linking liking, looks, and learning. *Teaching of Psychology, 34*(1), 5–10. https://doi.org/10.1080/00986280709336641

Guthrie, E. R. (1949). The evaluation of teaching. *Educational Record, 30*, 109–115.

Hamermesh, D. S., & Parker, A. M. (2005). Beauty in the classroom: Professors' pulchritude and putative pedagogical productivity. *Economics of Education Review, 24*(4), 369–376. https://doi.org/10.1016/j.econedurev.2004.07.013

Hessler, M., Pöpping, D. M., Hollstein, H., Ohlenburg, H., Arnemann, P. H., Massoth, C., . . . Wenk, M. (2018). Availability of cookies during an academic course session affects evaluation of teaching. *Medical Education, 52*(10), 1064–1072. https://doi.org/10.1111/medu.13627

Jackson, L. A., Hunter, J. E., & Hodge, C. N. (1995). Physical attractiveness and intellectual competence: A meta-analytic review. *Social Psychology Quarterly, 58*(2), 108–122. http://doe.org/10.2307/2787149

Kanazawa, S., & Kovarb, J. (2004). Why beautiful people are more intelligent. *Intelligence, 32*(3), 227–243. https://doi.org/10.1016/j.intell.2004.03.003

Keeley, J. W., English, T., Irons, J., & Henslee, A. M. (2013). Investigating halo and ceiling effects in student evaluations of instruction. *Educational and Psychological Measurement, 73*(3), 440–457. https://doi.org/10.1177/0013164412475300

Kelly-Woessner, A., & Woessner, M. C. (2006). My professor is a partisan hack: How perceptions of a professor's political views affect student course evaluations. *PS: Political Science & Politic, 39*(3), 495–501. https://doi.org/10.1017/S104909650606080X

Kelly-Woessner, A., & Woessner, M. C. (2008). Conflict in the classroom: Considering the effects of partisan difference on political education. *Journal of Political Science Education, 4*(3), 265–285. https://doi.org/10.1080/15512160802202789

Lahey, J. (2016, January 21). Just like performing magic. *The Atlantic, Education*. Retrieved from www.theatlantic.com/education/archive/2016/01/what-classrooms-can-learn-from-magic/425100

Marsh, H. W., & Hocevar, D. (1991). Students' evaluation of teaching effectiveness: The stability of mean rating of the same teachers over a 13-year period. *Teaching & Teaching Education, 7*(4), 303–314. https://doi.org/10.1016/0742-051X(91)90001-6

Marsh, H. W., & Ware, J. E. (1982). Effects of expressiveness, content coverage, and incentive on multidimensional student rating scales: New interpretations of the Dr. Fox effect. *Journal of Educational Psychology, 74*(1), 126–134. https://doi.org/10.1037/0022-0663.74.1.126

McPherson, M. A., Jewell, R. T., & Kim, M. (2009). What determines student evaluation scores? A random effects analysis of undergraduate economics classes. *Eastern Economic Journal, 35*, 37–51. https://doi.org/10.1057/palgrave.eej.9050042

Murray, H. G. (1983). Low-inference classroom teaching behaviors and student ratings of college teaching effectiveness. *Journal of Educational Psychology, 75*(1), 138–149. https://doi.org/10.1037/0022-0663.75.1.138

Naftulin, D. H., Ware, J. E., & Donnelly, F. A. (1973). The doctor fox lecture: A paradigm of educational seduction. *Journal of Medical Education, 48,* 630–635. Retrieved from https://adrianmarriott.net/logosroot/papers/DrFoxSpoof.pdf

Peer, E., & Babad, E. (2014). The doctor fox research (1973) revisited: "Educational seduction" ruled out. *Journal of Educational Psychology, 106*(1), 36–45. https://doi.org/10.1037/a0033827

Renaud, R. D., & Murray, H. G. (1996). Aging, personality, and teaching effectiveness in academic psychologists. *Research in Higher Education, 37*(3), 223–240. https://doi.org/10.1007/BF01730120

Shevlin, M., Banyard, P., Davies, M., & Griffiths, M. (2000). The validity of student evaluation of teaching in higher education: Love me, love my lectures? *Assessment & Evaluation in Higher Education, 25*(4), 397–405. https://doi.org/10.1080/713611436

Theall, M., & Franklin, J. (2001). Looking for bias in all the wrong places: A search for truth or a witch hunt in student ratings of instruction? *New Directions for Institutional Research, 27*(5), 45–56. https://doi.org/10.1002/ir.3

Thorndike, E. L. (1920). A constant error in psychological ratings. *Journal of Applied Psychology, 4*(1), 25–29.

Tom, G., Tong, S. T., & Hesse, C. (2010). Thick slice and thin slice teaching evaluations. *Social Psychology of Education, 13*(1), 129–136. https://doi.org/10.1007/s11218-009-9101-7

Trout, P. (1997). How to improve your teaching evaluation scores without improving teaching. *The Montana Professor, 7*(3). Retrieved from https://mtprof.msun.edu/Fall1997/HOWTORAI.html

Verbeeten, M. J., & van Hoof, H. B. (2007). Mandatory attendance policy and motivation among hospitality management students. *Journal of Hospitality & Tourism Education, 19*(1), 28–37. https://doi.org/10.1080/10963758.2007.10696880

Wachtel, H. K. (1998). Student evaluations of college teaching effectiveness: A brief review. *Assessment & Evaluation in Higher Education, 23*(2), 191–211. https://doi.org/10.1080/0260293980230207

Ware, J. E., & Williams, R. G. (1979). Seeing through the Dr. Fox effect: A response to Frey. *Instructional Evaluation, 3,* 6–10.

Ware, J. E., & Williams, R. G. (1980). A reanalysis of the Doctor Fox experiments. *Instructional Evaluation, 4,* 15–18.

Wilson, J. H., Beyer, D., & Monteiro, H. (2014). Professor age affects student ratings: Halo effect for younger teachers. *College Teaching, 62*(1), 20–24. https://doi.org/10.1080/87567555.2013.825574

Wilson, R. C., Dienst, E. R., & Watson, N. L. (1973). Characteristics of effective college teachers as perceived by their colleagues. *Journal of Educational Measure, 10*(1), 31–37. https://doi.org/10.1111/j.1745-3984.1973.tb00779.x

Wright, R. E. (2000). Student evaluations and consumer orientation of universities. *Journal of Nonprofit and Public Sector Marketing, 8*, 33–40. https://doi.org/10.1300/J054v08n01_04

Yermack, J., & Forsyth, D. R. (2016). Students' implicit theories of university professors. *Scholarship of Teaching and Learning in Psychology, 2*(3), 169–178. https://doi.org/10.1037/stl0000067

Youmans, R. J., & Jee, B. D. (2010). Fudging the numbers: Distributing chocolate influences student evaluations of an undergraduate course. *Teaching in Psychology, 34*(4), 245–247. https://doi.org/10.1080/00986280701700318

5   Are Students Truthful?

Do Students Tell the Truth When They Fill Out the Evaluations?

Joel teaches a freshman introductory class every year. He has described his interaction with the students in the class as "difficult." The evaluations from the class are typically lower than average, and Joel has diligently attempted to raise them. Every semester he studies the student comments carefully, looking for aspects of his teaching on which he could improve. Several times he has run across student comments that were simply not true, and on several occasions, he has had to include notes to the Professional Assessment Committee indicating comments were in error. He wonders if students are purposely lying or are just mistaken. He has never heard any of his colleagues discuss the issue and wonders if he is the only person with this potential problem.

Given the centrality of SET in establishing important elements of an instructor's career, it would seem reasonable to expect a great deal of research about the truthfulness of the respondents. Paradoxically, this aspect of SET has been studied perhaps less than any other factor related to the evaluations. It is almost as if no one had thought of it. The SET administrative procedures ironically question the honesty of the instructors, and even those who administer the forms, but never the honesty of the respondents (Stanfel, 1995; Wright, 2006).

Examples

Some students do have stronger reactions to instructors and classes than do others, and a corresponding stronger desire to express their views. As evidence of this, lower response rates to SET have been found to be associated with both higher and lower evaluations than larger response rates

(Bacon, Johnson, & Stewart, 2016). As previously shown, there is a strong halo effect on the evaluations, indicating students will ignore the content of individual questions while responding in a holistic fashion based on some overarching concern (Feeley, 2002; Tang & Tang, 1987; Orsini, 1988). As a demonstration, in an analysis of over 500 separate evaluations from a large online database, this writer found a correlation between the instructors' handwriting and adequate office hours of 0.64. Researchers looking at almost 7,000 professors' online evaluations found a correlation of about 0.60 between instructors' *"hotness"* and the quality of the class (Felton, Koper, Mitchell, & Stinson, 2004, 2008). There is evidence that some students will take the halo effect a step further and will report information on the evaluations that is not true (Clayson & Haley, 2011; Emery, Kramer, & Tian, 2003). Whether this is malicious or done purposely is not always evident.

The honesty problem was demonstrated in an experiment conducted by Stanfel (1995). The evaluation used by his university contained several questions that could be collaborated. Stanfel explained how the students were to be evaluated, and gave them a quiz to test their knowledge of his instruction. One hundred percent of the students were able to correctly outline exactly what his evaluation procedures were. In addition, the students signed documents indicating when they had received their graded work. In other words, students could not receive their graded material any earlier, and each student acknowledged that fact. How did the students later respond on the instructor evaluations? Only 3% of the students "strongly agreed" that the instructor had explained his evaluation procedure. Sixty-four percent either disagreed or "strongly" disagreed. Only 3% "strongly agreed" that assignments were handed back in a reasonable period; over 46% disagreed or "strongly" disagreed. Stanfel concluded the students either forgot what had been clearly presented to them, did not understand what the evaluation was asking, or they intentionally made false responses. He maintained the latter was the most logical explanation, but the previous explanations would also have called into question the accuracy of student responses.

Sproule (2000) recounts how 50% of his students in one class would not acknowledge work was returned "reasonably promptly" when *all* work was marked and returned the very next class period.

When students were asked if they ever intentionally used SET to reward or punish an instructor, 41% answered yes (Lin, 2008). Another study found students believe that 30% of all evaluations contain scores and/or written comments the responding student *knows* is untrue. Furthermore, the majority of students had no ethical problems with this deceit and did not feel that purposeful misreporting was a form of cheating (Clayson & Haley, 2011).

Two anecdotal accounts are warranted here; one negative and one positive. The writer once left the university a day early before a holiday break for family reasons. The syllabus clearly stated no roll would be taken in class and attendance was strictly voluntary. A guest speaker, who was an expert in the topic of the day, was invited to lecture the class. On the course evaluations, three students claimed they were "forced" to attend a class before a holiday, even though the instructor failed to show up. The claim was factually untrue and suggested a pattern of negative behavior of the instructor that was also untrue, but the fact that several students collectively made the claim added credence. The examples are not always negative. The writer once taught an elective course to seniors. No student was required to take the class and all students were thoroughly familiar with the instructor after three and half years of interaction. It is unlikely that any student who disliked the instructor would have taken the course. The class was held directly after the lunch hour across the campus from the instructor's office. That term, the instructor would meet with the campus chaplain and a sociology professor for lunch, and a vigorous debate was commonplace. The instructor realized he was regularly showing up to class a little late. On the college's SET was an unambivalent question; "Does the instructor show up to class on time?" As a test of the accuracy of student responses, the instructor purposely came to class a few minutes late the remainder of the term. On the evaluation, 100% of the students reported the instructor showed up to class "on time."

Evaluating Non-Existing Content

Some evidence suggests a majority of students, if asked, will evaluate presentations and instructors who do not exist. Emery et al. (2003) discussed a case in which a faculty member taught a course that had no lab, but the SET instrument asked students to evaluate labs with an added category stating the questions were "not applicable." Only 12 of 32 students marked "not applicable." The 20 evaluations of the non-existing lab lowered the overall evaluation below the college's average. Reynolds (1977) reported an incident when nearly 1,000 students completed an evaluation of a course in which there were ten invited speakers. One speaker never appeared. Nevertheless, 80% of the students evaluated the non-existing lecture, ranking it worse than six, but better than three. Some of the same students were shown a film in class, while others did not see the film. About 55% of the students who did not see the film evaluated it anyway, giving it a slightly above-average evaluation.

In a more subtle example, two classes were combined into one. One class was composed of honor students and the other was second-semester majors.

Both groups were in the same classroom and received the same lectures from the same instructor. For administration purposes, the evaluations were separated as if there had been two classes taught. The honors students rated the instructor and class higher than the majors on 19 of 22 measures, which may make sense, but the honors students also stated the exams were more representative of the material covered and that the instructor demonstrated more enthusiasm; both measures that should not be influenced by anything except being present in the class (Oliver-Hoyo, 2008).

Summary

1 Students will ignore the actual content of a question or statement on the evaluation by answering them in a manner consistent with a more global student concern or issue.
2 Some evidence suggests a majority of students will evaluate instruction and events they have never experienced.
3 Information is surprisingly limited on this topic, but the research that does exist is consistent in finding that a certain percentage of students will purposely falsify answers.

References

Bacon, D. R., Johnson, C. J., & Stewart, K. A. (2016). Nonresponse bias in student evaluations of teaching. *Marketing Education Review*, *26*(2), 93–104. https://doi.org/10.1080/10528008.2016.1166442

Clayson, D. E., & Haley, D. A. (2011). Are students telling us the truth? A critical look at the student evaluation of teaching. *Marketing Education Review*, *21*(2), 103–114. https://doi.org/10.2753/MER1052-8008210201

Emery, C. R., Kramer, T. R., & Tian, R. G. (2003). Return to academic standards: A critique of student evaluations of teaching effectiveness. *Quality Assurance in Education*, *11*(1), 37–46. http://doi.org/10.1108/09684880310462074

Feeley, T. H. (2002). Evidence of halo effects in student evaluations of communication instruction. *Communication Education*, *51*(3), 225–236. https://doi.org/10.1080/03634520216519

Felton, J., Koper, P. T., Mitchell, J., & Stinson, M. (2004). Web-based student evaluations of professors: The relations between perceived quality, easiness and sexiness. *Assessment & Evaluation in Higher Education*, *29*(1), 91–108. https://doi.org/10.1080/0260293032000158180

Felton, J., Koper, P. T., Mitchell, J., & Stinson, M. (2008). Attractiveness, easiness and other issues: Student evaluations of professors on Ratemyprofessors.com. *Assessment & Evaluation in Higher Education*, *33*(1), 45–61. https://doi.org/10.1080/02602930601122803

Lin, T. (2008, December 2). *Economic behavior in student ratings of teaching: Revenge or reward?* SSRN. http://dx.doi.org/10.2139/ssrn.1318177

Oliver-Hoyo, M. (2008). Two groups in the same class: Different grades. *Journal of College Science Teaching, 38*(1), 37–39. www.jstor.org/stable/42993234

Orsini, J. L. (1988, Summer). Halo effects in student evaluations of faculty: A case application. *Journal of Marketing Education, 10*, 38–45. https://doi.org/10.1177/027347538801000208

Reynolds, D. V. (1977). Faculty forum. *Teaching of Psychology, 4*(2), 82–83.

Sproule, R. (2000). Student evaluation of teaching: A methodological critique of conventional practices. *Educational Policy Analysis Archives, 8*(50), 1–23. https://doi.org/10.14507/epaa.v8n50.2000

Stanfel, L. E. (1995). Measuring the accuracy of student evaluations of teaching. *Journal of Instructional Psychology, 22*(2), 117–125.

Wright, R. E. (2006). Student evaluations of faculty: Concerns raised in the literature, and possible solutions. *College Student Journal, 40*(2), 417–422. Retrieved from www.researchgate.net/publication/307466136_Student_evaluations_of_faculty_Concerns_raised_in_the_literature_and_possible_solutions

6 Rigor, Grades, and How They Impact Student Evaluations

Do Academic Rigor and Grades Change the Evaluations?

Mattie is a senior professor within a few years of retirement. She teaches a core course in her department to undergraduates. The student grapevine describes her class as interesting and informative, but as a "killer." Mattie believes students are best served when they are best educated, and an educated person doesn't simply memorize but understands pertinent material. Her tests and quizzes are built around understanding and give almost no credit for memorized responses. The average letter grade in the class is seldom higher than 2.0, and As are reserved for truly outstanding work. Her administrators praise her for her academic rigor and have never suggested she change what she is doing in class. Her student evaluations are all over the board, resulting in an average only slightly above the departmental average. Mattie believes if she "gave away the store" and lowered her standards, her evaluations would rise.

Note: *The rigor-grade-evaluation topic was once extensively researched, but current studies, at least in the U.S., have become rarer. It is not known whether this has resulted from a lack of interest, a notion that the influence of these factors has been resolved, or if more sophisticated statistical techniques have made the topics irrelevant. Consequently, much of the research reviewed here will be from an earlier date. The rigor-grade-evaluation association remains, however, an important part of the SET debate.*

Many, like Mattie, hold the opinion that students will give lower evaluations to classes which are more difficult than normative courses. Some have even suggested that students will utilize SET as a means of punishing instructors who maintain high standards (Crumbley, Henry, & Kratchman, 2001; Pounder, 2007).

It is difficult to separate the effects of rigor and grades on the evaluations. In many cases, they are synonymous. Nevertheless, in an attempt to clarify certain issues, it is useful to look at each separately.

Rigor

Contradictory Findings

The literature on rigor and SET is full of contradictions. According to Cashin (1995), there is a correlation between rigor (defined as workload and difficulty) and the evaluations, but "contrary to faculty belief," the correlation is positive. As Greenwald and Gillmore (1997) pointed out, workload should be related to how much, on average, students learn, and learning is assumed to be positively related to grades and thus to the evaluations. Consequently, one would expect workload would be positively related to the evaluations. However, they found higher workloads were associated with lower grades, which was associated with lower evaluations. In another study of over 400 educators in Israel, the majority agreed that SET contributed to the improvement of teaching, but the majority also agreed that high demands in class would lead to lower evaluations (Nasser & Fresko, 2002). If the evaluations are valid, the instructors seem to be suggesting that lowering rigor would improve education.

Possible Explanations

Rigor-evaluation contradictions could be related to a number of normative issues. Rigor can be seen as having a linear or curvilinear relationship with performance (Marsh & Roche, 2000). Evaluations and rigor could positively be related up to a point and then negatively related after that point. In addition, the effects of rigor on the evaluations have been shown to be related to differences in students. Bacon and Novotny (2002) found lenient instructors would increase their evaluations by attracting low-achievement, striving students, but less so with students whom are highly motivated by achievement. Some other studies have shown students do not believe a demand for rigor is an important characteristic of a good teacher (Clayson, 2001, 2005a). In sum, students appear to have established norms for rigor which can vary widely. If perceived rigor is within those normative levels, for all practical purposes, rigor is ignored.

Rigor-evaluation contradictions have also been attributed to incomplete operational definitions and methodologies (Gaski, 1987; Howard & Maxwell, 1980; Marsh & Roche, 2000; Seiver, 1983). As suggested previously, the rigor of a class might not have a main effect on SET, but could be related to other factors which influence the evaluations, many of which would require more sophisticated statistical analysis to clarify. Clayson and Haley (1990) found rigor to be significantly associated with the student perception of learning, but was negatively linked to fairness, which made its total effect on the evaluation negative. Students admitted they would learn more in a rigorous class, but a class with this rigor would be unfair, and fairness appeared to be more important than learning. Marks (2000) essentially replicated this study and found a significant negative relationship between workload difficulty and fairness in grading, which in turn was significantly related to the overall evaluation.

Reputation of Class Difficulty and Grading Policies

Irrespective of other indices of rigor, students are attracted to classes that have a reputation for lenient grading (Carter, 2016). Wilhelm (2004) compared course evaluations and grading leniency as factors of business students choosing classes. A conjoint analysis showed, "students are 10 times more likely to choose a course with a lenient grader, all else being equal" (p. 24). Johnson (2003), after looking at the results of a large study completed at Duke University, concluded,

> The influence of grading policies on student course selection decision is substantial; when choosing between two courses within the same academic field, students are about twice as likely to select a course with an A- mean course grade as they are to select a course with a B mean course grade, or to select a B+ mean course grade over a B- mean course grade.
>
> (p. 193)

Grades

Many instructors believe there is a relationship between the grades they give and the evaluations students give to them. A survey conducted at an American university found over 65% of the surveyed faculty believed higher standards for grades would lower student evaluations (Birnbaum, 2000). When asked if the evaluation process encourages faculty to "water down" the content of their courses, 72% responded in the affirmative. Almost half of the faculty said they present less material in class than they used to, and about one-third said they have lowered standards for students to get a passing grade (only 7% said they had raised standards). Similar findings have consistently been found over a wide spectrum of both time and situations (Backer, 2012; Crumbley & Fliedner, 2002; Goldman,

1985; Simpson & Siguaw, 2000; Redding, 1998; Ryan, Anderson, & Birchler, 1980).

> An actual, and apparently sincere, student endorsement from an online evaluation site read,
> **"I didn't read much but still got an A. really great professor."**

Historical Development

Although education scholars admitted there was a grade-evaluation association (Braskamp & Ory, 1994; Marsh & Dunkin, 1992), many continued to state that rigorous grading standards did not significantly change student teacher evaluations, especially if other variables like rigor and prior student interest were taken into account (Cashin, 1995; Marsh & Dunkin, 1992; Kaplan, Mets, & Cook, 2000; Marsh & Roche, 2000). Marsh and Roche (1999) referred to the idea that academic rigor would result in lower student teacher evaluations as a "presumption" that was not supported by the research. As evidence, they stated the grade-evaluation association was too small ($r = 0.20$, approximately 4% of the variance) to be an important bias. Almost a decade later, Marsh (2007) stated, "Whereas a grading-leniency effect may produce *some* bias in SETs, support for this suggestion is weak, and the size of such an effect is likely to be insubstantial" (p. 357).

Contradictory research findings, however, indicated this positive assessment may have been oversimplified. In an early meta-analysis, Cohen (1981) reported a correlation of 0.43 between achievement (measured by grades) and the evaluations, but found no correlation ($r = -0.02$) between "difficulty" and achievement. Other findings continued to find a grade-evaluation association. Gillmore and Greenwald (1999) reported that out of six published studies that manipulated grading leniency in classrooms, all found higher evaluations from students in the more lenient conditions. Expected grades were found to create a highly significant difference in the evaluations of business instructors (Goldberg & Callahan, 1991). The final course grade was also shown to have a negative impact on the evaluations (Bharadwaj, Futrell, & Kantak, 1993). Marsh, Hau, Chung, and Siu (1997) recognized a highly significant difference between the grades students indicated they received from those instructors chosen as "good" and "poor" teachers. In an attempt to not contradict early assumptions, they interpreted this finding as a reflection of course mastery and as more evidence for the validity of the instruments, even though they found that course grades were positively correlated with the students' perception of learning, but negatively correlated with rigor.

More recent findings tend to come from areas that joined the SET debate later. Currently, evidence for a negative grade-evaluation association has been coming from international studies. The connection has not only been identified in the United States, but also in Taiwan (Chen, Wang, & Yang, 2017), Australia (Backer, 2012), and Belgium (Brockx, Spooren, & Mortelmans, 2011) with very similar results.

The research, in some ways, has become more nuanced. Anyone who has experience with SET will note that some instructors' evaluations appear to be highly influenced by the grades they give, while others do not appear to have any connection. There is some evidence that grades effects, like those with rigor, may interact with other variables (Brockx et al., 2011; Culver, 2010). For example, it has been found that the students' perception of the instructor's personality modifies the impact of grades on the SET. If an instructor is seen as "caring" and gives high grades, then the instructor is given higher evaluations. If the instructor is seen as uncaring, then the instructor gets little credit for a good grade, but is blamed for poor grades (Gotlieb & Milliman, 2005).

Theories (Grade Relationships to SET)

As it stands now, the major debate about the grade-evaluation association is not whether it exists, but what causes it. Historically, five theories were proposed (Clayson, Frost, & Sheffet, 2006; Greenwald & Gillmore, 1997; Marsh & Roche, 1997, 2000; Stumpf & Freedman, 1979).

1 *Leniency:* Lenient professors will get better evaluations than more rigorous graders. It is important to this hypothesis to recognize, "it is not the grades per se that influence SETs, but the leniency with which grades are assigned" (Marsh & Roche, 2000, p. 204).
2 *Interaction with prior characteristics:* An apparent leniency effect exists, but it is not real. It is a result of either a statistical artifact of other determining variables, or is largely modified to the point of practical insignificance by other variables (Seiver, 1983). These variables could include the rigor of the instructor's grading policies (Powell, 1977; Stumpf & Freedman, 1979), class workloads (Greenwald & Gillmore, 1997; Marsh & Roche, 2000; Schwab, 1976), and prior student interest in the class (Marsh & Roche, 2000).
3 *Teaching effectiveness:* Teaching effectiveness influences both the evaluations and grades. Good instructors create positive learning environments that are reflected in more positive grades. Defenders of the evaluation system tend to support this hypothesis (Cohen, 1981; Marsh & Roche, 1997) with some statistical support (Seiver, 1983).

4   *Motivation:* The students' level of motivation influences both evaluations and grades. More highly motivated students are expected to do better academically and to appreciate the efforts of the instructor more. Certain instructors may attract motivated students or be better at motivating students than other instructors (Greenwald & Gillmore, 1997).

5   *Attribution and cognitive dissonance:* Since learning and achievement are difficult to evaluate, students may infer the ability of the instructor to teach and their level of learning from the grade they receive. This can be looked at in two different ways. Greenwald and Gillmore (1997) describe attribution as grades providing information to students about course quality and ability. Thus, a student getting a good grade would attribute it to good performance and to good teaching. A poor grade would indicate a lack of learning and a poor instructor. Marsh and Roche (2000) looked at attribution as a psychological variable that predisposes students to attribute good grades to themselves and poor grades to an external source, i.e., the teacher (see Maurer, 2006). An example was shown in a study of Spanish language students at an American university (Zabaleta, 2007). A correlation greater than 0.4 was found between the evaluations and the grades of the students in the bottom tenth percentile, but no correlation in the students in the top tenth percentile of grades. The overall correlation was 0.35 (t = 10.39).

6   *Reciprocity:* At first glance, reciprocity appears to be a leniency explanation, but it is distinctly different. The reciprocity hypothesis states that students have a tendency to give the instructor what they receive. Students reward instructors who reward them and punish those who apparently punish them (Cho, Baek, & Cho, 2015). The general level of grading leniency of the instructor is not relevant, only the individual student's reaction to their grade. This difference is also reflected in methodology. As Marsh and Roche (2000) point out, the appropriate case for a study of leniency is a class. The appropriate case to study reciprocity is the student. These are statistically distinct concepts (Clayson, 2007; Stumpf & Freedman, 1979).

Evidence

Leniency or Reciprocity

Greenwald and Gillmore (1997) addressed most of these hypotheses. The teaching effectiveness explanation was the easiest to deal with. The hypothesis generated by this theory would be supported by a between-class positive grade-evaluation association, but invalidated by a within-class positive correlation. Both of these have been found. Numerous studies conducted before 1977 were reviewed by Stumpf and Freedman (1979). The weighted average of these studies was r = 0.39 for the grade-evaluation relationship when the correlation was calculated between-classes and r = 0.11 when the correlation was calculated within-classes. Further, the theory would be damaged by a difference in correlations between relative vs. absolute grades, if halo effects exist within-class but not with between-class evaluations (Tang & Tang, 1987; Orsini, 1988), and negative between-class correlations between grades and workloads-difficulty, all of which have been found (Greenwald & Gillmore, 1997). The halo effects and the negative grade-workload-difficulty correlations create problems for the motivation theories. Attribution is a well-established psychological reality and should be found in the students' explanation of the source of their grades, but it only partially explains why it should be associated with valid evaluations. The only hypothesis supported by all the data is the reciprocity theory.

Johnson's (2003) well-regarded study found strong evidence of a leniency effect by using between-class data. However, he also found evidence of a grade-evaluation effect with between-student data, suggesting the presence of a reciprocity effect. Lin (2009) also found a reciprocity effect that was summarized in the language of economics as, "meaning that the higher the marginal cost of taking the class, the lower the student will rate the professor" (p. 1735).

This writer conducted an unpublished study utilizing the data from 700 students taken from an online source. Knowing that the actual given grade accounted for 25% of the evaluation's variance and since women are punished more for a violation of norms, it came as little surprise to find the grade-evaluation relationship was stronger for women instructors than for men (r = 0.60 for women, r = 0.46). There was a perfect rank order correlation between the average students' letter grades and the average evaluation, a result replicated by Culver (2010). The rank order was maintained between grades and even within grades (i.e., the average evaluation of a student receiving a C+ was higher than the average evaluation of students receiving a C).

Another study (Clayson et al., 2006) found, even after ten weeks of instruction, students continued to change their evaluations systematically with changes in their expected grades. The effect was found to be universal and not related to the instructors' general level of leniency, or to student characteristics. In other words, the very best and the very worst students (as measured by their own demographics) reacted in a similar manner. Note what the study implies. Since the instructor's characteristics (in this case, leniency) were unlikely to change in the middle of a term, the students are not reacting to a predisposition of the instructor, but are reacting individually to changes in their own grade.

These studies suggest the grade-evaluation association is largely due to a reciprocity effect, and it has the potential of creating important differences in the student evaluations. As previously noted, this has led some to conclude that the grade-evaluation relationship has been one of the seminal factors creating grade inflation. "In the case of university teaching, rewarding employee teaching performance by a piece-rate, SET-based pay system, the consequence is not necessarily improved organizational performance. Instead, comparing and paying university faculty for higher SETs appears to encourage inflated grades" (Langbein, 2008, p. 427).

Grading Standards

Researchers have used both final grades and expected grades as independent variables, but how do students relate these to SET? One hypothesis suggests that students perceive a certain standard of fairness based on how rewards and costs are shared across a significant group. If they don't find fairness in this comparison, it affects the evaluations (Tripp, Jiang, Olson, & Graso, 2019). Part of this is related to the average grade in the class (Blackhart, Peruche, DeWall, & Joiner, 2006) and to the distribution (variance) of the grades. As would be expected, poorer students respond more positively to a "tight distribution" of expected grades than do good students (Matos-Diaz & Ragan, 2010). Some research suggests it is not the expected grade in itself that effects the evaluations, but the gap between expected grades and the cumulative grade point average of the students (Isely & Singh, 2005). This goes to the genesis of expected grades, which are almost lawfully different from actual grades (Chistianens, Spooren, Mortelmans, & Van Loon, 2014; Kennedy, Lawton, & Plumlee, 2002). It appears students have a fairly accurate perception of their grades, but consistently expect to receive a grade that is roughly the average between their actual grade and a norm established outside of class (Clayson, 2005b). The students, therefore, are reacting individually to what they might consider to be an unfair violation of norms.

This hypothesis is reinforced by what appears to be contradictory effects of GPA on the evaluations. Before the mid-1980s, it was thought students with higher grade point averages generally gave higher evaluations, which was advanced as an indicator of the validity of SET (see Centra, 1993; Marsh, 1987, for a review). However, more recent findings have shown only small global effects of GPA, and these effects vary greatly between instructors and courses (Griffin, Hilton, Plummer, & Barret, 2014). In one study, the authors summed up their apparently contradictory findings by stating, "if students feel that they are treated fairly by the instructor, their GPA will not affect their evaluation of teaching" (Badri, Abdulla, Kamali, &

Dodeen, 2006, p. 53). In other words, GPA can be seen as an indicator of norms rather than evidence that better students give higher evaluations, and thus as a norm, might influence students' perception of fairness.

Other Related Issues

The magnitude of the rigor-grade-evaluation relationship depends upon how it is measured (Clayson, 2004; Feldman, 1997). If data is collected after the class is completed, the correlations between the variables become more robust. Grades can also be seen as an indicator of perceived learning instead of a biasing factor. If learning and SET are positively linked, and grades, rigor, and learning are strongly related, then a rigor-grade-evaluation association can be seen as an indicator of SET validity. However, as will be discussed in a future chapter, and based on more current information, this is a questionable assumption. A meta-analysis by Sitzmann, Ely, Grown, and Bauer (2010) reviewed 137 separate studies involving almost 17,000 students and found a weighted mean correlation of only 0.27 between objective measures of learning and the student assessment of learning (7% of the variance). They concluded, "These results suggest that self-assessed knowledge is generally more useful as an indicator of how learners feel about a course than as an indicator of how much they learned from it." In the next chapter, we shall see that SET and learning may be unrelated.

Stepping Back to Basics

When looking at grade effects on the evaluations, it is instructive to step back and review the basics. *Classes do not fill out student teaching evaluations; students do* (Clayson, 2009). While Marsh and Roche's (1997, 2000) insistence that classes are the appropriate cases for studying leniency is accurate, the requirement comes with inherent statistical problems that make such studies problematic. Insisting on class-mean data as cases, without sophisticated statistical control, increases the probability of Type I errors. Leniency can appear to exist when it does not and the findings are severely confounded by reciprocity effects. Statistical modelling shows the magnitude of the leniency effects to be influenced by the variance of the grades given, skewness of responses, the size of the class, boundary effects, and response scales. Larger introductory classes, where grade inflation is controlled and students show wide differences in ability, would mathematically expect larger apparent grade-evaluation effects than smaller, more homogenous classes with a small variation of high grades. This would be accurate even if the true leniency effect in both types of classes was identical (Clayson, 2007). In other words, researchers looking at a large number of intro classes in a more difficult academic area would expect to find a larger leniency effect than a similar study of advanced education-related classes. The difference could simply be a statistical artifact.

Importance to Faculty

Irrespective of the actual effect of grades and rigor on SET, if faculty believe a negative association exists, the belief alone will change behavior. Crumbley and Fliedner (2002) surveyed accounting administrators. Almost 40% of the respondents were aware of instructors who had reduced their grading standards and course work content to improve SET scores.

Summary

1. Rigor is a controversial variable in the evaluation debate. Some have maintained there is a positive relationship between rigor and SET. Others claim the relationship is negative.
2. Rigor is an interactive variable. Its impact on the evaluations appears to be due to its effect on grades, fairness, and even student personality.
3. The relationship between grades and the evaluations has traditionally been assumed to be low, but more recent research has found a substantial association.
4. There is some evidence that part of the grade-evaluation relationship is due to the leniency of the instructor and psychological attribution. However, the reciprocity effect is the only hypothesis which conforms to *all* the data. In blunt terms, students have a tendency to give an instructor what they thought they received.
5. The cause of the rigor-grade-evaluation relationship is complex, but it appears to be most related to the perception of a violation of expected norms.

References

Backer, E. (2012). Burnt at the student evaluation stake – the penalty for failing students. *e-Journal of Business Education & Scholarship of Teaching*, 6(1), 1–13. Retrieved from www.ejbest.org/

Bacon, D. R., & Novotny, J. (2002). Exploring achievement striving as a moderator of the grading leniency effect. *Journal of Marketing Education*, 24(2), 4–14. https://doi.org/10.1177/0273475302241002

Badri, M., Abdulla, M., Kamali, M., & Dodeen, H. (2006). Identifying potential biasing variables in student evaluation of teaching in a newly accredited business program in the UAE. *International Journal of Educational Management*, 20(1), 43–59. https://doi.org/10.1108/09513540610639585

Bharadwaj, S., Futrell, C. M., & Kantak, D. M. (1993, Summer). Using student evaluations to improve learning. *Marketing Education Review*, *3*, 16–21. https://doi.org/10.1080/10528008.1993.11488406

Birnbaum, M. H. (2000). *A survey of faculty opinions concerning student evaluation of teaching*. Retrieved from http://psych.fullerton.edu/mbirnbaum/faculty3.htm

Blackhart, G. C., Peruche, M., DeWall, C. N., & Joiner, T. E. (2006). Faculty forum: Factors influencing teaching evaluations in higher education. *Teaching of Psychology*, *33*(1), 37–39. https://doi.org/10.1207/s15328023top3301_9

Braskamp, L. A., & Ory, J. C. (1994). *Assessing faculty work: Enhancing individual and institutional performances*. San Francisco: Jossey-Bass.

Brockx, B., Spooren, P., & Mortelmans, D. (2011). Taking the grading leniency story to the edge. The influence of student, teacher, and course characteristics on student evaluations of teaching in higher education. *Educational Assessment, Evaluation and Accountability*, *23*, 289–306. https://doi.org/10.1007/s11092-011-9126-2

Carter, R. E. (2016). Faculty scholarship has a profound positive association with student evaluations of teaching – Except when it doesn't. *Journal of Marketing Education*, *38*(1), 18–36. https://doi.org/10.1177/0273475315604671

Cashin, W. E. (1995). *Student ratings of teaching: The research revisited* (IDEA Paper No. 32). Publication of the Center for Faculty Evaluation & Development, Division of continuing Education, Kansas State University. Retrieved from https://files.eric.ed.gov/fulltext/ED402338.pdf

Centra, J. A. (1993). *Reflective faculty evaluations: Enhancing teaching and determining faculty effectiveness*. San Francisco: Jossey-Bass.

Chen, C. Y., Wang, S., & Yang, Y. (2017). A study of the correlation of the improvement of teaching evaluation scores based on student performance grades. *International Journal of Higher Education*, *6*(2), 162–168. https://files.eric.ed.gov/fulltext/EJ1140507.pdf

Chistianens, W., Spooren, P., Mortelmans, D., & Van Loon, F. J. A. (2014). Students' perceptions of learning, course grades, and student evaluation of teaching: An empirical analysis. *The International Journal of Assessment and Evaluation*, *20*(3), 13–21. http://doi.org/ 10.18848/2327-7920/CGP/v20i03/48350

Cho, D., Baek, W., & Cho, J. (2015). Why do good performing students highly rate their instructors? Evidence from a natural experiment. *Economics of Education Review*, *49*, 172–179. https://doi.org/10.1016/j.econedurev.2015.10.001

Clayson, D. E. (2001). Academic rigor and the student teacher evaluation process: Student perceptions. In S. Van Auken & R. P. Schlee (Eds.), *Riding the wave of innovation in marketing education*. Marketing Educators' Association Conference Proceedings (pp. 19–22). Madison, WI: Omnipress Press. Retrieved from www.marketingeducators.org/2001-proceedings

Clayson, D. E. (2004). A test of the reciprocity effect in the student evaluation of instructors in marketing classes. *Marketing Education Review*, *14*(2), 11–21. https://doi.org/10.1080/10528008.2004.11488863

Clayson, D. E. (2005a). Within-class variability in student-teacher evaluations: Example and problems. *Decision Sciences Journal of Innovative Education*, *3*(1), 109–124. https://doi.org/10.1111/j.1540-4609.2005.00055.x

Clayson, D. E. (2005b). Performance overconfidence: Metacognitive effects or misplaced student experience. *Journal of Marketing Education, 27*(2), 11–21. https://doi.org/10.1177/0273475304273525

Clayson, D. E. (2007). Conceptual and statistical problems of using between-class data in educational research. *Journal of Marketing Education, 29*(1), 34–38. https://doi.org/10.1177/0273475306297383

Clayson, D. E. (2009). Student evaluation of teaching: Are they related to what students learn? A meta-analysis and review of the literature. *Journal of Marketing Education, 31*(1), 16–30. https://doi.org/10.1177/0273475308324086

Clayson, D. E., Frost, T. F., & Sheffet, M. J. (2006). Grades and the student evaluation of instruction: A test of the reciprocity effect. *Academy of Management Learning & Education, 5*(1), 52–65. https://doi.org/10.5465/amle.2006.20388384

Clayson, D. E., & Haley, D. A. (1990, Fall). Student evaluations in marketing: What is actually being measured? *Journal of Marketing Education, 12*, 9–17. https://doi.org/10.1177/027347539001200302

Cohen, P. A. (1981). Student ratings of instruction and student achievement: A meta-analysis of multi-section validity studies. *Review of Educational Research, 51*, 281–309. https://doi.org/10.3102/00346543051003281

Crumbley, D. L., & Fliedner, E. (2002). Accounting administrators' perception of student evaluation of teaching (SET) information. *Quality Assurance in Education, 10*(4), 213–222. https://doi.org/10.1108/09684880210446884

Crumbley, D. L., Henry, B. K., & Kratchman, S. H. (2001). Students' perceptions of the evaluation of college teaching. *Quality Assurance in Education, 9*(4), 197–207. https://doi.org/10.1108/EUM0000000006158

Culver, S. (2010). Course grades, quality of student engagement, and students' evaluation of instructor. *International Journal of Teaching and Learning in Higher Education, 22*(3), 331–336. https://files.eric.ed.gov/fulltext/EJ938568.pdf

Feldman, K. A. (1997). Identifying exemplary teachers and teaching: Evidence from student ratings. In R. P. Perry & J. C. Smart (Eds.), *Effective teaching in higher education: Research and practice* (pp. 368–395). New York: Agathon.

Gaski, J. F. (1987). On 'construct validity of measures of college teaching effectiveness'. *Journal of Educational Psychology, 79*, 326–330. https://doi.org/10.1037/0022-0663.79.3.326

Gillmore, G. M., & Greenwald, A. G. (1999). Using statistical adjustment to reduce biases in student ratings. *American Psychologist, 54*(7), 518–519. (Original data published: Greenwald, Anthony G. 1991. *American Psychologist, 52*, 1182–1186. https://doi.org/10.1037/0003-066X.54.7.518

Goldberg, G., & Callahan, J. (1991July–August). Objectivity of student evaluations of instructors. *Journal of Education for Business*, 377–378. https://eric.ed.gov/?id=EJ430770

Goldman, L. (1985). The betrayal of the gatekeepers: Grade inflation. *Journal of General Education, 37*, 97–121. https:// www.jstor.org/stable/27797025

Gotlieb, J., & Milliman, R. (2005, Winter). Do student grades affect student numeric ratings of marketing professors? Applying attribution theory to help answer this question. *Journal for Advancement of Marketing Education, 7*, 11–26. Retrieved

from https://pdfs.semanticscholar.org/3c78/950fc8c355b551333791e9f95b12053
2eb70.pdf
Greenwald, A. G., & Gillmore, G. M. (1997). Grading leniency is a removable contaminant of student ratings. *American Psychologist*, *52*(11), 1209–1217. https://doi.org/10.1037/0003-066X.52.11.1209
Griffin, T. J., Hilton, J., Plummer, K., & Barret, D. (2014). Correlation between grade point averages and student evaluation of teaching scores: Taking a closer look. *Assessment & Evaluation in Higher Education*, *39*(3), 339–348. https://doi.org/10.1080/02602938.2013.831809
Howard, G. S., & Maxwell, S. E. (1980). Correlation between student satisfaction and grades: A case of mistaken causation? *Journal of Educational Psychology*, *72*, 810–820. https://doi.org/10.1037/0022-0663.72.6.810
Isely, P., & Singh, H. (2005). Do higher grades lead to favorable student evaluations? *The Journal of Economic Education*, *36*(1), 29–42. https://doi.org/10.3200/JECE.36.1.29-42
Johnson, V. E. (2003). *Grade inflation: A crisis in college education*. New York: Springer.
Kaplan, M., Mets, L. A., & Cook, C. E. (2000). *Questions frequently asked about student ratings forms: Summary of research findings*. Retrieved from www.crit.umich.edu/crit.faq.html
Kennedy, E. J., Lawton, L., & Plumlee, E. L. (2002). Bliss ignorance: The problem of unrecognized incompetence and academic performance. *Journal of Marketing Education*, *24*(3), 243–252. https://doi.org/10.1177/0273475302238047
Langbein, L. (2008). Management by results: Student evaluation of faculty teaching and the mis-measurement of performance. *Economics of Education Review*, *27*, 417–428. https://doi.org/10.1016/j.econedurev.2006.12.003
Lin, T. (2009). Endogenous effects of midterm grades and evaluations: A simultaneous framework. *Economics Bulletin*, *29*(3), 1731–1742. Retrieved from https://pdfs.semanticscholar.org/59f3/d368e89ba707148095b8f5349cc666e1c66c.pdf
Marks, R. B. (2000). Determinants of student evaluations of global measures of instructor and course value. *Journal of Marketing Education*, *22*(2), 108–119. https://doi.org/10.1177/0273475300222005
Marsh, H. W., & Dunkin, M. (1992). Students' evaluations of university teaching: A multidimensional perspective. In J. C. Smart (Ed.) *Higher education: Handbook of theory and research* (Vol. 8, pp. 143–233). New York: Agathon.
Marsh, H. W., Hau, K., Chung, C., & Siu, T. L. (1997). Students' evaluations of university teaching: Chinese version of the students' evaluations of educational quality instrument. *Journal of Educational Psychology*, *89*(3), 568–572. https://doi.org/10.1037/0022-0663.89.3.568
Marsh, H. W., & Roche, L. A. (1997). Making students' evaluations of teaching effectiveness effective. *American Psychologist*, *52*(11), 1187–1197. https://doi.org/10.1037/0003-066X.52.11.1187
Marsh, H. W., & Roche, L. A. (1999). Reply upon set research. *American Psychologist*, *54*(7), 517–518. https://doi.org/10.1037/0003-066X.54.7.517

Marsh, H. W., & Roche, L. A. (2000). Effects of grading leniency and low workload on students' evaluations of teaching: Popular myth, bias, validity, or innocent bystanders? *Journal of Educational Psychology*, *92*(1), 202–228. https://doi.org/10.1037/0022-0663.92.1.202

Marsh, W. H. (1987). Students' evaluations of university teaching: Research findings, methodological issues, and directions for future research. *International Journal of Educational Research*, *11*(3), 253–388. https://doi.org/10.1016/0883-0355(87)90001-2

Marsh, W. H. (2007). Do university teachers become more effective with experience? A multilevel growth model of students' evaluations of teaching over 13 years. *Journal of Educational Psychology*, *99*(4), 775–790. https://doi.org/10.1037/0022-0663.99.4.775

Matos-Diaz, H., & Ragan, J. (2010). Do student evaluations of teaching depend on the distribution of expected grade? *Education Economics*, *18*(3), 317–330. https://doi.org/10.1080/09645290903109444

Maurer, T. W. (2006). Cognitive dissonance or revenge? Student grades and course evaluations. *Teaching of Psychology*, *33*(3), 176–179. https://doi.org/10.1207/s15328023top3303_4

Nasser, F., & Fresko, B. (2002). Faculty views of student evaluation of college teaching. *Assessment & Evaluation in Higher Education*, *27*(2), 187–198. https://doi.org/10.1080/02602930220128751

Orsini, J. L. (1988, Summer). Halo effects in student evaluations of faculty: A case application. *Journal of Marketing Education*, *10*, 38–45. https://doi.org/10.1177/027347538801000208

Pounder, J. S. (2007). Is student evaluation of teaching worthwhile? An analytical framework for answering the question. *Quality Assurance in Education*, *15*(2), 178–191. https://doi.org/10.1108/09684880710748938

Powell, R. W. (1977). Grades, learning, and student evaluation of instructors. *Research in Higher Education*, *7*, 193–205. https://doi.org/10.1007/BF00991986

Redding, R. E. (1998). Students' evaluation of teaching fuel grade inflation. *American Psychologist*, *53*(11), 1227–1228. https://doi.org/10.1037/0003-066X.53.11.1227

Ryan, J. J., Anderson, J. A., & Birchler, A. B. (1980). Student evaluation: The faculty responds. *Research in Higher Education*, *12*(4), 317–333. https://doi.org/10.1007/BF00976185

Schwab, D. P. (1976). *Manual for the course evaluation instrument*. Madison: University of Wisconsin, School of Business.

Seiver, D. A. (1983). Evaluations and grades: A simultaneous framework. *The Journal of Economic Education*, *14*(3), 32–38. https://doe.org/10.1080/00220485.1983.10845024

Simpson, P. M., & Siguaw, J. A. (2000). Student evaluations of teaching: An exploratory study of the faculty response. *Journal of Marketing Education*, *22*(3), 199–213. https://doi.org/10.1177/0273475300223004

Sitzmann, T., Ely, K., Grown, K. G., & Bauer, K. N. (2010). Self-assessment of knowledge: A cognitive learning of affective measure? *Academy of Management Learning & Education*, *9*(2), 169–191. https://doi.org/10.5465/amle.9.2.zqr169

Stumpf, S. A., & Freedman, R. D. (1979). Expected grade covariation with student ratings of instruction: Individual versus class effects. *Journal of Educational Psychology, 71*(3), 293–302. https://doi.org/10.1037/0022-0663.71.3.293

Tang, T. L., & Tang, T. L. (1987, Spring). A correlation study of students' evaluations of faculty performance and their self-ratings in an instructional setting. *College Student Journal, 21*, 90–97. https://files.eric.ed.gov/fulltext/ED279981.pdf

Tripp, T. M., Jiang, L., Olson, K., & Graso, M. (2019). The fair process effect in the classroom: Reducing the influence of grades on student evaluations of teachers. *Journal of Marketing Education, 41*(3), 173–184. https://doi.org/10.1177/0273475318772618

Wilhelm, W. B. 2004. The relative influence of published teaching evaluations and other instructor attributes on course choice. *Journal of Marketing Education, 26*, 17–30. https://doi.org/10.1177/0273475303258276

Zabaleta, F. (2007). The use and misuse of student evaluations of teaching. *Teaching in Higher Education, 12*(1), 55–76. https://doi.org/10.1080/13562510601102131

7 The Association Between Student Learning and Student Evaluations

Is Student Learning Associated With the Evaluations?

Brittany gets excellent evaluations. They are almost perfect. Last year she was informed she ranked in the top 98th percentile of all instructors at her university. She admitted to a friend that being a superior teacher was part of her self-concept. She is proud of the teaching awards she has earned. Brittany works hard to make sure she is on the cutting edge of her class topics and is always looking for new ways to make her classes better. Brittany's office door is always open. She enjoys her interaction with students, and takes pride in their success. One afternoon while she was visiting with a colleague, he happened to mention that he had finished reviewing a well-organized and provocative paper that found no relationship between SET and learning. Further, the paper referenced other research which had similar results. Brittany was shocked. "That can't be true," she said. "Obviously, students will learn more from good teachers. Besides, when I was in graduate school, we were told the evaluations were very strongly correlated with learning. What are you going to say in your review?"

Brittany's point is well taken. Of all the definitions that could be given about what "good" or "effective" teaching is, most would assume it is related to what students learn. As Cohen (1981) affirmed, "Even though there is a lack of unanimity on a definition of good teaching, most researchers in this area agree student learning is the most important criterion of teaching effectiveness" (p. 283). This presumption has not changed over the years. "But whatever it is, effective teaching should promote student learning: *ceteris paribus;* students of an effective instructor should have better learning outcomes than students of an ineffective instructor have" (Boring, Ottoboni, & Stark, 2016, p. 3).

However, the relationship between SET and learning would be more accurately suggested by asking a slightly different question. *Would the results of SET procedures differentiate between instructors from whom students are learning, as opposed to instructors from whom students are not learning?* And even if that dichotomous judgment is realized, can the association between student learning and SET procedures result in information that could pragmatically be utilized in instructional feedback leading to more student learning?

Definition

It is important to know how the word "learning" is used in the following discussion. While it might be true that students could learn a great deal in a class about study habits, open-mindedness, and even courage and fortitude, learning here is defined in terms of performance. Academic courses exist for a purpose. A calculus class is taught so students will know more calculus. In other words, the class should create gains in the skills and knowledge of students related to calculus. Students taking a Spanish class should gain reading and speaking ability in Spanish. In addition, learning, "reflects a change over time, not a state at a particular moment in time" (Bacon, 2016, p. 3). Learning, as used in this context, is a gain in performance related to the purpose of a class. It does not refer to the students' perception of learning. The two are related (Bacon, 2016; Clayson, 2009), but the perception of learning accounts for only about 12% of the variance of actual learning (Sitzmann, Ely, Grown, & Bauer, 2010).

Historical Development

Researchers in the past reported finding a positive relationship between learning and student ratings of instructors (Baird, 1987; Lundsten, 1986; Marlin & Niss, 1980). Dowell and Neal (1982) did a careful review of the literature and concluded the correlation between learning and the evaluations was about 0.20 to 0.26, accounting for about 4–6% of the variance. Nevertheless, prior to the mid-70s, about half of studies had found no correlation, or a negative correlation, between some measures of learning and the evaluations (Sullivan & Skanes, 1974). Other data, however, was even more disturbing. The most widely cited and debated example was reported by Rodin and Rodin (1972) in *Science*, who found a negative correlation of -0.75. About the same time, a study from the UK, utilizing the evaluations of over 30,000 students, found a correlation no different from zero between the evaluations and student learning in economics (Attiyeh &

Lumsden, 1972). A more recent meta-analysis (Clayson, 2009) found no published findings after 1990 that contained a statistically significant positive association between learning and the evaluations. This study declared that the association between SET and student learning decreased as measurements of learning became more objective, and as research methods of controlling for secondary variables became more sophisticated. The research concluded that while there was a relationship between SET and *perceived* learning, there was none between objective measures of learning and SET. In fact, the students' perception of learning in graded assignments has been shown to be associated with SET, even when actual learning and the evaluations were weakly related (Boring et al., 2016; O'Connell & Dickinson, 1993). In another study, what engineering students learned was carefully measured with pre- and posttests and computer-controlled applications. The authors (Mohanty, Gretes, Flowers, Algozzine, & Spooner, 2005) reported, "No relationship was demonstrated between learning and traditional course evaluation outcomes" (p. 139). The latest meta-analysis again found no association between SET and learning (Uttl, White, & Gonzalez, 2017). These authors concluded, "Despite more than 75 years of sustained effort, there is presently no evidence supporting the widespread belief that students learn more from professors who receive higher SET ratings" (p. 31 of manuscript).

Learning Disassociated From SET

The expectation of an association between SET and learning retained by many instructors and administrators does not appear to be strongly held by students. Other concerns seem more important to them than learning. In an interesting experimental study, identical lectures were given by simulated instructors who differed by gender and race (Basow, Codos, & Martin, 2013). Differences in SET were not related to differences in learning. Students performed better (learned more) from male than from female simulated instructors, with no difference in SET. At the same time, minority instructors had significantly higher evaluations than white instructors with corresponding lower learning scores. Delucchi and Pelowski (2000) found a strong relationship between how much students liked their instructor and the overall evaluation, but no relationship between liking their instructor and the students' perception of learning. Even more to the point, it appears many students and instructors don't associate learning with the evaluations. In a study of accounting professors who were asked what variables influenced SET scores, the phrase "How much students learn" was rated 11th behind such things as enthusiasm, grading policy, and how "nice" the instructor is seen by students. Less than half (42%) rated learning as being

Student Learning and Student Evaluations 67

of major importance to SET scores (Crumbley & Reichelt, 2009). Accounting administrators were a bit more positive, rating "student learning" as the eighth most important factor affecting scores, behind enthusiasm, instructor niceness, and course difficulty (Crumbley & Fliedner, 2002). It is interesting to note that although 87% of accounting professors reported SET instruments were used to determine tenure decisions, and 70% said the evaluations were used for merit pay decisions (Crumbley & Reichelt, 2009), about half of accounting administrators said they were either unsure student learning was related to SET or they did not think learning was related to student evaluations (Crumbley & Fliender, 2002). Even in the education of medical practitioners, when students were asked what qualities they liked most in an instructor, the word "learning" was never directly mentioned (Jahangiri & Mucciolo, 2008).

SET and Deep Learning

If learning is seen as an improvement in future performance, then the research suggests learning may actually be negatively related to SET (Kornell & Hausman, 2016). In a study of accounting students, a statistically significant negative relationship existed between student evaluations of their instructors in intro classes and how well they performed in a subsequent class, even when controlling for student GPA and ACT scores (Yunker & Yunker, 2003). Johnson (2003), utilizing a university-wide database, reported "stringent grading is associated with higher levels of achievement in follow-up courses" (p. 161), but stringent grading was strongly associated with lower evaluations. At the United States Air Force Academy, students in calculus classes, in which learning can be objectively measured, gave higher evaluations to instructors of classes in which they were getting higher grades, but lower evaluations to instructors who produced students who did well in subsequent calculus classes. The authors concluded, "the correlation between introductory calculus professor value added in the introductory and follow-on courses is negative. Students appear to reward contemporaneous course value added . . . but punish deep learning" (Carrell & West, 2010, p. 429). Consistent with this, they found inexperienced instructors got better evaluations in introductory classes than did more seasoned instructors, who produced students who did better in subsequent classes. These results have been found in other venues. In a large study in Italy, the authors (Braga, Paccagnella, & Pellizzari, 2014) state,

> we find that, on average, students evaluate positively classes that give high grades and negatively classes that are associated with high grades in subsequent classes. . . . Overall, our results cast serious doubts on the

validity of students' evaluations of professors as measures of teaching quality or effort.

(p. 30)

Researchers at The Ohio State University found a similar effect. They operationally defined learning not as the grades in a class, but the grades in subsequent classes. Looking at a data set containing over 48,000 individual evaluations, they found no association with these grades and the evaluations taken in previous classes (Weinberg, Hashimoto, & Fleisher, 2009). One of the keys to these findings is randomization. The negative findings generally came from schools in which students could not select the instructor or select specific subsequent classes. This is an important distinction. Without randomization, the relationship between evaluations in subsequent classes is confounded by ecological factors.

Exceptions

When students enroll in a class designed to prepare them to pass an external instrument of importance, students may acknowledge teachers who prepare them well. For example, accounting students take certain classes to prepare them to take the CPA exam. One study found a small but statistically significant association between the course evaluation and student grades on an external posttest which had serious consequences for the students (Beleche, Fairris, & Marks, 2012).

Complicating Alternatives

There is some evidence to suggest that even if an association is found between learning and the evaluations, it may not reflect a first-order relationship. That is to say, finding or not finding a student-learning/instructor-evaluation association for many students may result from relationships which are fundamentally spurious. There are two lines of reasoning for this contention.

First, while learning could be a positive outcome sought by many students, the time and effort to learn could be seen negatively by the same students, creating a conflict between student motivations. Appleton-Knapp and Krentler (2006) observed, "The best learning strategies are often the least liked by students" (p. 262). (One is reminded of the cynical remark sometimes attributed to journalists, "If you make people think they're thinking, they'll love you, but if you really make them think, they'll hate you.")[1]

Second, there is another potential problem which has gone almost entirely unreported. It can be demonstrated by a grossly ungrammatical sentence:

"I learned ya." Instructors do not "learn" their students. It is not clear if how much a student learns can be attributed to an instructor. Learning experiences are complex and typically stretch over long periods of time, which could contain numerous events both with and without any interaction with an instructor. As Ching (2018) states, "It is, therefore, difficult to determine whether a single class experience or the collective sum of the semester's learning encounters contribute to the SET ratings" (p. 73). As stated in another source, "Isolating students' course achievement at one point in time or gains over time that are attributable directly to teaching is nearly impossible" (Berk, 2013, p. 32). In a paradoxical study of chemistry classes (Elliott, 1950) conducted with students who were born almost 100 years ago, a relationship was found between the students' perceptions of the knowledge of their instructors and an objective measure of their instructors' knowledge. "The students in these recitation sections, then, were significantly able to distinguish instructors who know more about chemistry from those who knew less" (Doyle, 1975, p. 54). However, it was also found the association between the instructors' knowledge and what the students learned was negative. In other words, the students did less well on objective measures in sections taught by the instructors who knew the most. In another interesting study, this from the field of physics, what students knew about certain principles in physics was compared before and after a class was completed. The researchers (Halloun & Hestenes, 1985) found the common-sense beliefs held by the students at the beginning of the term were significant predictors of their performance in class, but class instruction induced only a small change toward correcting errors. The students' failure to improve was not related to their instructors' class evaluations. The researchers concluded, "The *basic knowledge gain under conventional instruction is essentially independent of the professor* [italics theirs]" (p. 1048).

In addition, the relationship between learning and instruction might be complicated by still another factor. Hopefully it is rare, but it is not always evident the students are learning *anything* from the class or instructor. A survey of 1,827 college students discovered, "The average literacy of U.S. college students was generally the same regardless of how long students had been in college, their enrollment status, or the number of postsecondary institutions they attended" (Baer, Cook, & Baldi, 2006, p. 6). In other words, the number of instructors and classes students had was generally unrelated to any change in literacy. In a small study in marketing education, there was no relationship between the number of marketing courses a student had completed and the student's level of marketing knowledge (Raska, Weisenbach-Keller, & Shaw, 2012). As Weinberg et al. (2009) concluded after a careful development of statistical methods for relating learning to the evaluations, "the characteristics of instructors that matter the most [for learning] are unobservable" (pp. 21–22). As a reminder, mathematically, a constant always has a correlational association with any variable of zero.

Response

Some defenders of SET now admit the evaluations are not measures of student learning. Some, like Linse (2017), have stated the SET evaluations "have never intended to serve as a proxy for learning" (p. 55). While this statement is accurate, as demonstrated by the previous discussion, it is also misleading. Irrespective of the intent, most practitioners assume "effective" teaching *is* associated with learning.

Anecdotal evidence is always questionable, but it can be illustrative. The following is an experience related by Simpson and Siguaw (2000).

> At one small university we know of, graduating seniors in the business college realized an increase in their standing on a nationally scaled exam in finance from the 13th percentile to the 97th percentile. The most likely explanation for this dramatic rise in learning was the addition of a finance faculty member solely responsible for teaching all required finance courses. Despite this amazing learning outcome, this instructor consistently placed in the lowest third of all faculty in the college. This anecdotal evidence indicates that the current SET measures may not be sufficiently assessing the critical variable of teaching effectiveness in terms of student learning, yet the measure is instrumental in evaluating faculty.
>
> (p. 219)

Summary

1 Although students generally do not list learning as an important characteristic of good instruction, students' perception of learning is positively related to SET.
2 The literature suggests a possible relationship between learning and SET could have existed in the past. Generational and cultural change might have altered the relationship. Research published after 1990 has found little or no evidence of a connection between student learning and SET.
3 There is currently a negative correlation between deep learning and SET. Students from classes with high SET scores tend to do more poorly in subsequent classes.
4 There is limited evidence to suggest students will reward learning if learning is needed to achieve an important goal outside of class, such as passing a standardized exam.

5 One explanation of the lack of association between learning and SET posits that it is difficult to attribute learning to any given event or individual. In addition, students may not be learning much from any instructor, irrespective of how those instructors are evaluated. The correlation of a constant with any variable is zero.
6 Overall, research from numerous sources and venues have found the correlation between objective learning and SET is essentially zero. The evaluations *will not* differentiate between instructors whose students are learning and instructors whose students are not learning.
7 Although there have been attempts to minimize the importance of learning on the SET process, the lack of association between SET and learning presents a serious challenge to the validity of the evaluations.

Note

1 Quote is attributed to the American humorist Don Marquis.

References

Appleton-Knapp, S. L., & Krentler, K. A. (2006). Measuring student expectations and their effects on satisfaction: The importance of managing student expectations. *Journal of Marketing Education*, *28*(3), 254–264. https://doi.org/10.1177/0273475306293359

Attiyeh, R., & Lumsden, K. G. (1972). Some modern myths in teaching economics: The U. K. experience. *American Economic Review*, *62*, 429–433. www.jstor.org/stable/1821578

Bacon, D. R. (2016). Reporting actual and perceived student learning in education research. *Journal of Marketing Education*, *38*(1), 3–6. https://doi.org/10.1177/0273475316636732

Baer, J. D., Cook, A. L., & Baldi, S. (2006). *The literacy of America's college students: National survey of American college students*. Washington, DC: American Institutes for Research.

Baird, J. S. (1987). Perceived learning in relation to student evaluation of university instruction. *Journal of Educational Psychology*, *79*(1), 90–91. https://doi.org/10.1037/0022-0663.79.1.90

Basow, S. A., Codos, S., & Martin, J. L. (2013). The effects of professors' race and gender on student evaluations and performance. *College Student Journal*, *47*(2), 352–363. Retrieved from www.ingentaconnect.com/content/prin/csj/2013/00000047/00000002/art00011

Beleche, T., Fairris, D., & Marks, M. (2012). Do course evaluations truly reflect student learning? Evidence from an objectively graded post-test. *Economics of Education Review*, *31*(5), 709–719. https://doi.org/10.1016/j.econedurev.2012.05.001

Berk, R. A. (2013). *Top 10 flashpoints in student ratings and the evaluation of teaching*. Sterling VA: Stylus.

Boring, A., Ottoboni, K., & Stark, P. B. (2016). Student evaluation of teaching (mostly) do not measure teaching effectiveness. *ScienceOpen*. https://doi.org/10.14293/S2199-1006.1.SOR-EDU.AETBZC.v1

Braga, M., Paccagnella, M., & Pellizzari, M. (2014). Evaluating students' evaluations of professors. *Economic Education Review, 41*, 71–88. https://doi.org/10.1016/j.econedurev.2014.04.002

Carrell, S. E., & West, J. E. (2010). Does professor quality matter? Evidence from random assignment of students to professors. *Journal of Political Economy, 118*(3), 409–432. https://doi.org/10.1086/653808

Ching, G. (2018). A literature review on the student evaluation of teaching: An examination of the search, experience, and credence qualities of SET. *Higher Education Evaluation and Development, 12*(2), 63–84. https://doi.org/10.1108/HEED-04-2018-0009

Clayson, D. E. (2009). Student evaluation of teaching: Are they related to what students learn? A meta-analysis and review of the literature. *Journal of Marketing Education, 31*(1), 16–30. https://doi.org/10.1177/0273475308324086

Cohen, P. A. (1981). Student ratings of instruction and student achievement: A meta-analysis of multi-section validity studies. *Review of Educational Research, 51*, 281–309. https://doi.org/10.3102/00346543051003281

Crumbley, D. L., & Fliedner, E. (2002). Accounting administrators' perception of student evaluation of teaching (SET) information. *Quality Assurance in Education, 10*(4), 213–222. https://doi.org/10.1108/09684880210446884

Crumbley, D. L., & Reichelt, K. J. (2009). Teaching effectiveness, impression management, and dysfunctional behavior: Student evaluation of teaching control data. *Quality Assurance in Education, 17*(4), 377–392. https://doi.org/10.1108/09684880910992340

Delucchi, M., & Pelowski, S. (2000). Liking or learning? The effect of instructor likability and student perceptions of learning on overall ratings of teaching ability. *Radical Pedagogy, 2*(2). Retrieved from http://radicalpedagogy.icaap.org/content/issue2_2/delpel.html

Dowell, D. B., & Neal, J. A. (1982). A selective review of the validity of student ratings of teaching. *Journal of Higher Education, 53*(1), 51–62. https://doi.org/10.1080/00221546.1982.11780424

Doyle, K. O. (1975). *Student evaluation of instruction*. Lexington, MA: Lexington Books.

Elliott, D. H. (1950). Characteristics and relationships of various criteria of college and university teaching. *Purdue University Studies in Higher Education, 70*, 5–61.

Halloun, I. A., & Hestenes, D. (1985). The initial knowledge state of college physics students. *American Journal of Physics, 53*(11), 1053–1055. https://doi.org/10.1119/1.14030

Jahangiri, L., & Mucciolo, T. W. (2008). Characteristics of effective classroom teachers as identified by students and professionals: A qualitative study. *Journal of Dental Education, 72*(4), 484–493. Retrieved from www.medianet-ny.com/Research-Study-Jahangiri_Mucciolo-April-2008.pdf

Johnson, V. E. (2003). *Grade inflation: A crisis in college education*. New York: Springer.

Kornell, N., & Hausman, H. (2016, April). Do the best teachers get the best ratings? *Frontiers in Psychology, 7,* 570. https://doi.org/10.3389/fpsyg.2016.00570/full

Linse, A. R. (2017). Interpreting and using student ratings data: Guidance for faculty serving as administrators and on evaluation committees. *Studies in Educational Evaluation, 54,* 94–106. https://doi.org/10.1016/j.stueduc.2016.12.004

Lundsten, N. L. (1986). Student evaluations in a business administration curriculum: A marketing viewpoint. *AMA Developments in Marketing Science, 9,* 169–173. https://doi.org/10.1007/978-3-319-11101-8_36

Marlin, J. W., & Niss, J. F. (1980, Spring). End-of-course evaluations as indicators of student learning and instructor effectiveness. *The Journal of Economic Education, 16*–27. https://doi.org/ 10.1080/00220485.1980.10844950

Mohanty, G., Gretes, J., Flowers, C., Algozzine, B., & Spooner, F. (2005). Multi-method evaluation of instruction in engineering classes. *Journal of Personnel Evaluation in Education, 18*(2), 139–151. https://doi.org/10.1007/s11092-006-9006-3

O'Connell, R. W., & Dickinson, D. J. (1993). Student ratings of instruction as a function of testing conditions and perceptions of amount learned. *Journal of Research and Development in Education, 27*(1), 18–23. https://eric.ed.gov/?id=EJ478565

Raska, D., Weisenbach-Keller, E., & Shaw, D. (2012). Curriculum alignment for improving learning outcomes. In S. Bharadwaj & J. Hulland (Eds.), *Marketing theory and applications, 2012 AMA Winter Educators' Conference* (Vol. 23, p. 318–319). Chicago: AMA.

Rodin, M., & Rodin, B. (1972, September 29). Student evaluation of teachers. *Science, 177,* 1164–1166. https://doi.org/ 10.1080/00220485.1973.10845375

Simpson, P. M., & Siguaw, J. A. (2000). Student evaluations of teaching: An exploratory study of the faculty response. *Journal of Marketing Education, 22*(3), 199–213. https://doi.org/10.1177/0273475300223004

Sitzmann, T., Ely, K., Grown, K. G., & Bauer, K. N. (2010). Self-assessment of knowledge: A cognitive learning of affective measure? *Academy of Management Learning & Education, 9*(2), 169–191. https://doi.org/10.5465/amle.9.2.zqr169

Sullivan, A. M., & Skanes, G. R. (1974). Validity of student evaluations of teaching and the characteristics of successful instructors. *Journal of Educational Psychology, 66*(4), 584–590. https://doi.org/10.1037/h0036929

Uttl, B., White, C. A., & Gonzalez, D. W. (2017). Meta-analysis of faculty's teaching effectiveness: Student evaluation of teaching ratings and student learning are not related. *Studies in Educational Evaluation, 54,* 22–42. https://doi.org/10.1016/j.stueduc.2016.08.007

Weinberg, B. A., Hashimoto, M., & Fleisher, B. M. (2009). Evaluating teaching in higher education. *The Journal of Economic Education, 40*(3), 227–261. https://doi.org/10.3200/JECE.40.3.227-261

Yunker, P. J., & Yunker, J. (2003). Are student evaluations of teaching valid? Evidence from an analytical business core course. *Journal of Education for Business, 78*(6), 313–317. https://doi.org/10.1080/08832320309598619

8 Student Evaluations and the Improvement of Instruction

Do the Evaluations Improve Instruction?

Because of her position as Associate Dean of the college, Mary has access to years of SET outcomes from her faculty. As she was looking over the data, she failed to see any improvement in the average scores over time. Visiting with her dean, she remarked, "Over the last decade, the average SET scores have stayed the same. In fact, last year they were actually lower than they were 10 years ago." The dean replied, "Well, students are students. I suppose what they want hasn't changed much." Mary shook her head, "Yes, but this is what bothers me. Right in our faculty handbook, under the section outlining our SET procedures, we justify them by saying their main purpose is to improve the quality of instruction. Our students, however, are saying there is no improvement. What are we doing wrong?"

Mary is assuming the evaluation of a procedure can lead to an improvement in that procedure. However, there are a number of caveats implied in this assumption, the two most important being: Was the evaluation a valid measure of the procedure? And was the strategy employed to utilize the assessment information applied properly for improvement?

One of the reasons stated for employing a system of teaching evaluations is to improve teaching quality and effectiveness (Gaillard, Mitchell, & Vahwere, 2006; Palmer, 2012), and it is stated by some compilers that SET fulfills this function (Benton & Ryalls, 2016). Moreover, it would be logical to assume such a relationship. As stated by Linask and Monks (2018), "Indeed, if experience helps build human capital, then it may be appropriate to consider experience as a component of teaching effectiveness" (Footnote 7). However, as noted in a previous chapter, experience does not always appear to improve teaching performance as measured by SET. Since the evaluations are ubiquitous, it also implies years of experience with the evaluation instruments do not improve instruction either.

History

The research before 1970 led Centra (1972) to conclude, "There is some evidence that student feedback does indeed have a positive effect on teaching performance, although the evidence is far from conclusive" (p. 3). Centa had found there was no improvement of teaching with student SET feedback except for instructors who had an "unrealistic" view of their own teaching ability. He wrote, "regardless of the particular college, subject area of the course, sex of the instructor, or the number of years the instructor had taught, the feedback did not appear to produce a difference" (p. 29). What many have seen as the standard for the improvement hypothesis was an analysis conducted by Cohen (1980), who stated, "This meta-analysis showed that for the most part student-rating feedback has made a modest but significant contribution to the improvement of college teaching" (p. 336). This conclusion was reinforced more recently by a survey of Canadian instructors that concluded the evaluations were "marginally valuable" in improving instruction (Beran & Rokosh, 2009). Cohen's earlier conclusion, however, was not without its problems. The sample of papers was relatively small and only three of nine "comparisons" made by the study were statistically significant. Indeed, as with much of the older studies, direct tests of the improvement hypothesis resulted in mixed results. Some research has shown the SET improved teaching quality over time (Davidovitch & Soen, 2006; Penny, 2003), but again, the change appears to be small. Carle (2009) found, on average, the improvement amounted to a 0.01 increase per semester on a five-point scale. In the length of a career (30 years), that would amount to an increase of only 0.6 on the same scale. Others (Campbell & Bozeman, 2007; Kember, Leung, & Kwan, 2002) found no evidence of significant improvement. One investigation looked at the evaluations over a period of four years. Of the 25 different academic departments studied, only three showed any significant change, and those changes were negative. The study concluded there was no evidence the evaluations contributed to any improvement in the quality of teaching (Kember et al., 2002).

Implications

These findings seem to imply that experience does not help an instructor become a better teacher. Miron (1988) found years of teaching experience had only a modest effect on the relationship between instructors' self-ratings of their classes and the ratings given by students. In fact, beginning teachers were more accurate in judging their own instruction (as seen by students) than were more experienced teachers, and new teachers have been found to get higher evaluations than more experienced instructors (Carrell & West, 2010). Clayson and Haley (2011) instructed students to directly address the issue. They asked, "Do you think that instructors who are evaluated become better teachers?" Two-thirds of the students said "yes." The students were also asked if they thought the faculty and administrators read the written comments on the evaluations. There was no statistical relationship between the students' opinion about the usefulness of the evaluation and whether or not they thought they were actually read. In other words, the students believed SET improved instruction in some global sense, but did not relate that to anything specific. This seems to sum up the feelings of many faculty and administrators who suggest the SET system is necessary by alluding to vague and ethereal performance improvements, which they might have never measured.

Consensus

A type of compromising consensus seems to have developed among SET researchers. Many continue to believe the evaluations improve instruction (Cohen, 1980; Marsh & Roche, 1997; Overall & Marsh, 1979; Wachtel, 1998), but their use by themselves will not improve the quality of teaching without external feedback (Seldin, 1993; Wachtel, 1998; Wilson, 1986). As Marsh (1984) put it, "studies suggest feedback, coupled with a candid discussion with an external consultant, can be an effective intervention for the improvement of teaching effectiveness" (p. 746). While proposing a system of utilizing the evaluations to improve instruction, Smith (2008, p. 519) wrote,

> Student evaluation requires staff to interpret the results themselves is, in this author's opinion, unlikely to lead to improvements in teaching because staff who use the data are typically expert in neither (a) the theories of evaluation and evaluation measurement, nor (b) the theories of teaching and learning or the ways these might be measured.

However, apparently not all consultation is equally useful (Penny & Coe, 2004), and even with an external consultant, "potentially valuable feedback will be much less useful if there is no extrinsic motivation for faculty to improve" (Marsh, 1984, p. 747). As outlined by Spooren, Brockx, and Mortelmans (2013, p. 623), "Consultative feedback should consist of more than simply interpreting the results and providing advice for teaching improvement." Moreover, this warning implied, "SET ultimately does not achieve the goal of providing useful information to an important stakeholder, with the ultimate goal of improvement" (p. 623).

Instead of using consultants, one alternative methodology is to improve instruction by requiring teachers to undergo a process that would certify their competency. In the field of nursing, a certification exam was developed to demonstrate that a nurse educator had a high level of knowledge and competence. However, the certification was not required to teach. Grobe (2017) looked at the SET scores of certified nurse instructors compared to non-certified instructors. No statistically significant difference was found between the two.

Larger Concerns

Finding little relationship between SET utilization and improved teaching raises perplexing questions because it implies college-level instruction improves little with practice. Further, they raise the issue of why an evaluation needs to be combined with an *outside* expert to show improvement. It has even been suggested that university-level instructors are not "qualified to interpret such results [of SET] validly" (Aleamoni, 1999, p. 160). Does this suggest, as proposed by Smith's (2008) faculty ignorance hypothesis, that information for improvement provided by the evaluations is hidden from the object of the evaluation, and only becomes known when interpreted by a trained and "outside" consultant? Did the evaluations not provide the information needed by the instructor, and if so, what was the evaluation measuring? Instead of addressing these questions directly, some have suggested SET does improve instruction, but traditional methodologies have not been sufficient to identify it (L'Hommedieu, Menges, & Brinko, 1990). All of this raises a logical problem which led Becker and Watts (1999, p. 347) to ask, "How can something that has little or no information value for the agent have great information value for the principle?"

There are other issues. Utilizing SET to improve instruction assumes evaluation results could be modified, even from one administration to the next, and positive change would be expected from the student feedback. However, as indicated in previous discussions, the evidence seems to indicate that SET results do not generally change significantly over long periods of time. The consistency, in fact, has been utilized as an argument for SET reliability. In addition, does SET measure what an instructor does, i.e., the act of teaching, or who the instructor is? If it measures what an instructor does, then it should be relatively easy for an instructor to modify the evaluations, even without external help. On the other hand, if the measures are intrinsic to the instructor, the evaluations would be expected to be much harder to change.

Summary

1. Advocates of the SET process maintain the evaluations will improve instruction for individual instructors *if* they are combined with interpretation and coaching of an outside consultant.
2. On average, repeated administrations of SET does not appear to be related to significant improvements of instructional quality, as measured by SET.

References

Aleamoni, L. M. (1999). Student rating myths versus research facts from 1924 to 1998. *Journal of Personnel Evaluation in Education, 13*(2), 153–166. https://doi.org/10.1023/A:1008168421283

Becker, W. E., & Watts, M. (1999). How departments of economics evaluate teaching. *American Economic Review, 89*, 344–349. Retrieved from https://pubs.aeaweb.org/doi/pdf/10.1257/aer.89.2.344

Benton, S. L., & Ryalls, K. R. (2016). *Challenging misconceptions about student ratings of instruction* (IDEA PAPER No. 58). Manhattan, KS: The IDEA Center. Retrieved from https://files.eric.ed.gov/fulltext/ED573670.pdf

Beran, T. N., & Rokosh, J. L. (2009). Instructors' perspectives on the utility of student ratings of instruction. *Instructional Science, 37*(2), 171–184. https://doi.org/10.1007/s11251-007-9045-2

Campbell, J. P., & Bozeman, W. C. (2007). The value of student ratings: Perceptions of students, teachers, and administrators. *Community College Journal of Research and Practice, 32*(1), 13–24. https://doi.org/10.1080/10668920600864137

Carle, A. C. (2009). Evaluating college students' evaluations of a professor's teaching effectiveness across time and instruction mode (online vs. face-to-face) using a multilevel growth modeling approach. *Computers & Education, 53*(2), 429–435. https://doi.org/10.1016/j.compedu.2009.03.001

Carrell, S. E., & West, J. E. (2010). Does professor quality matter? Evidence from random assignment of students to professors. *Journal of Political Economy, 118*(3), 409–432. https://doi.org/10.1086/653808

Centra, J. A. (1972). *Two studies on the utility of student ratings for instructional improvement* (SIR Report No. 9). Princeton, NJ: Educational Testing Service.

Clayson, D. E., & Haley, D. A. (2011). Are students telling us the truth? A critical look at the student evaluation of teaching. *Marketing Education Review, 21*(2), 103–114. https://doi.org/10.2753/MER1052-8008210201

Cohen, P. A. (1980). Effectiveness of student-rating feedback for improving college instruction: A meta-analysis. *Research in Higher Education, 13*(4), 321–341. https://doi.org/10.1007/BF00976252

Davidovitch, N., & Soen, D. (2006). Using students' assessments to improve instructors' quality of teaching. *Journal of Further and Higher Education, 30*(4), 351–376. https://doi.org/10.1080/03098770600965375

Gaillard, F. D., Mitchell, S. P., & Vahwere, K. (2006). Students, faculty, and administrators perception of students evaluations of faculty in higher education business schools. *Journal of College Teaching & Learning, 8*(3), 77–90. https://doi.org/10.19030/tlc.v3i8.1695

Grobe, J. L. (2017). *Comparing student evaluations of certified and non-certified nurse educators* (Order No. 10640245). Available from ProQuest Dissertations & Theses A&I. (1972084835). Retrieved from https://search.proquest.com/docview/1972084835?accountid=14691

Kember, D., Leung, D. Y. P., & Kwan, K. P. (2002). Does the use of student feedback questionnaires improve the overall quality of teaching? *Assessment & Evaluation in Higher Education, 27*(5), 411–425. https://doi.org/10.1080/0260293022000009294

L'Hommedieu, R., Menges, R. J., & Brinko, K. T. (1990). Methodological explanations for the modest effects of feedback from student ratings. *Journal of Educational Psychology, 82*(2), 232–241. https://doi.org/10.1037/0022-0663.82.2.232

Linask, M., & Monks, J. (2018). Measuring faculty teaching effectiveness using conditional fixed effects. *The Journal of Economic Education, 49*(4), 324–339. https://doi.org/10.1080/00220485.2018.1500957

Marsh, H. W. (1984). Students' evaluation of university teaching: Dimensionality, reliability, validity, potential biases, and utility. *Journal of Educational Psychology, 76*(5), 707–754. https://doi.org/10.1037/0022-0663.76.5.707

Marsh, H. W., & Roche, L. A. (1997). Making students' evaluations of teaching effectiveness effective. *American Psychologist, 52*(11), 1187–1197. https://doi.org/10.1037/0003-066X.52.11.1187

Miron, M. (1988). Students' evaluation and instructors' self-evaluation of university instruction. *Higher Education, 17*, 175–181. https://doi.org/10.1007/BF00137970

Overall, J. U., & Marsh, H. W. (1979). Midterm feedback from students: Its relationship to instructional improvement and students' cognitive and affective outcomes. *Journal of Educational Psychology, 71*(6), 856–865. https://doi.org/10.1037/0022-0663.71.6.856

Palmer, S. (2012). Student evaluation of teaching: Keeping in touch with reality. *Quality in Higher Education, 18*(3), 297–311. https://doi.org/10.1080/13538322.2012.730336

Penny, A. R. (2003). Changing the agenda for students' views about university teaching: Four shortcoming of SRT research. *Teaching in Higher Education, 8*(3), 399–441. https://doi.org/10.1080/13562510309396

Penny, A. R., & Coe, R. (2004). Effectiveness of consultation on student ratings feedback: Meta-analysis. *Review of Educational Research, 74*(2), 215–253. https://doi.org/10.3102/00346543074002215

Seldin, P. (1993, July). The use and abuse of student ratings of professors. *Chronicles of Higher Education, 21*, A40.

Smith, C. (2008). Building effectiveness in teaching through targeted evaluation and response: Connecting evaluation to teaching improvement in higher education. *Assessment & Evaluation in Higher Education, 33*(5), 517–533.

Spooren, P., Brockx, B., & Mortelmans, D. (2013). On the validity of student evaluation of teaching: The state of the art. *Review of Educational Research, 83*(4), 598–642. https://doi.org/10.3102/0034654313496870

Wachtel, H. K. (1998). Student evaluations of college teaching effectiveness: A brief review. *Assessment & Evaluation in Higher Education, 23*(2), 191–211. https://doi.org/10.1080/0260293980230207

Wilson, R. C. (1986). Improving faculty teaching: Effective use of student evaluations and consultants. *The Journal of Higher Education, 57*(2), 196–211. https://doi.org/10.1080/00221546.1986.11778762

9 Challenging the Statistical Reliability of Student Evaluations

Are the Evaluations Statistically Reliable?

Lucinda is also an associate dean. Recently, a young faculty member was denied tenure based primarily on the results of the student evaluations. The rejected faculty member sued the university. Lucinda was asked to speak for and defend the college and the evaluations in court. She read most of the summaries of SET. They almost uniformly stated the SET instruments were reliable. The background material from her own university stated their instrument was also judged to have reliability. After she carefully presented her evidence in court, the rejected faculty member's attorney stood, looked at her and smiled. "How do we know the instruments are not reliability wrong?" he asked. Lucinda was taken aback. Wasn't reliability the foundation of any good instrument? Didn't it indicate the instrument had validity?

Lucinda did review the literature properly. SET is thought to be remarkably reliable. The controversy instead revolves around what is meant by the term and what it implies.

Definition

In its simplest form, reliability is the ratio of the variance in any measure due only to what the instrument claims to measure with the total variance of the instrument or scale.

$$r_{11} = \frac{\sigma^2_{true}}{\sigma^2_{total}}$$

In this form, reliability can range from zero, when there is no variance created by the true measure, to one, when all variance is created only by the true measure. Ascertaining the true variance is problematic when creating an instrument, such as a SET inventory, which supposedly measures a hypothetical construct. Consequently, it can be approached from several directions, each emphasizing different methodological concerns.

Reliability can be seen as an indicator of stability, accuracy, or reproducibility. Churchill and Brown (2004) clarified this by stating reliability was obtained when measurement was consistent from the same construct across time, different evaluators, or across different items forming the measure. This is stated in a more rigorous fashion by Krippendorff (2011), "reliability is the extent to which different methods, research results, or people arrive at the same interpretations of facts" (p. 94). In actual practice, this has historically been done by looking at the association of inter-rater, test-retest, parallel forms, and/or internal consistency measures. The problem with these applications is that each is capable of producing acceptable reliability scores from invalid instruments. Consequently, when ascertaining validity is the primary issue, Hayes and Krippendorff (2007) argue reproducibility is the strongest and most feasible test. In fact, if an instrument is valid, the key to reliability is the agreement between individual independent observers.

SET and Types of Reliability

The evaluation instruments are extraordinarily reliable when looking at class averages (Feldman, 1983; Cashin, 1995; Marsh & Roche, 1997) or consistency of scales (Zhao & Gallant, 2012). Some evaluation forms have created inter-item and inter-form reliabilities between 0.70 to 0.91 (Al-Eidan, Baig, Magzoub, & Omair, 2016; Sixbury & Cashin, 1995), leading some consultants to suggest forms creating reliability coefficients less than 0.70 be viewed with caution (Cashin, 1995).

As suggested in the previous section, reliability can also be looked at in terms of stability. A longitudinal study (Overall & Marsh, 1980) compared the ratings at the end of a course with the ratings given by students a year later and found a correlation of 0.83. This finding is reinforced by the results of a careful investigation by Marsh and Hocevar (1991). They reviewed a study by Feldman (1983) in which student evaluations of teaching effectiveness were found to be so consistent that they were only weakly related to seniority. Marsh and Hocevar (1991) investigated this suggestion by looking at 195 teachers from 31 different academic departments who taught 6,024 classes over a period of 13 years. They found in their longitudinal study that for both undergraduate and graduate-level courses, there were almost no changes over time in the means for any of nine content-specific dimensions, overall course ratings, or instructor ratings. The results between ratings and experience were essentially linear and not the result of a "U" type relationship. The findings were consistent for teachers who had little, moderate, or extensive amounts of experience at the beginning of the study. They concluded that over a 13-year longitudinal period, teaching effectiveness as perceived by students was stable.

Further research, however, has indicated the consistency of the evaluations is over class averages and not necessarily from agreement among individual class members. Further, it has been found that the correlation between the same instructor teaching the same class is between 0.70 and 0.80, but for the same instructor teaching two different classes, the correlations range from 0.33 to 0.48 (Gillmore, Kane, & Naccarato, 1978), indicating that knowing the present evaluations from a class can account for about 50–60% of the variability in the evaluations if the same class is taught again by the same instructor, but the knowledge of the instructors' present evaluations would account for only about 10–20% of the variability of teaching a new class. This is evidence that not all the variation accounted for in the correlation analysis can be attributed to the instructor. A considerable portion of it is attributable to a class effect. Gillmore et al. (1978) found about 40% of the variation in their study could be attributed to the teaching effect, 6% to a specific class effect, and the remaining 54% to unexplained interactions. Since these correlations are from class averages of the same instructor, the data implies a considerable amount of inter-class (i.e., individual student rater) variability exists. To minimize these effects, Marsh and Roche (1997) suggest that using data from individuals instead of class averages is "inappropriate."

Yet this approach covers up an interesting phenomenon. Follman (1984) reported a consistent 20% of teachers were rated as the *very* best and the *very* worst instructors by members of the same class – a finding reported consistently from grade school through graduate programs. This writer once asked 98 business students questions about trust in the classroom. One question read, "Have you ever had a teacher who you thought was an excellent teacher that some of your friends thought was a terrible teacher?" Seventy-six percent answered "yes." In other words, the evaluations seem to have a certain amount of between-class reliability, but seem to suffer from within-class or inter-student inconsistency. Further, it has been found that students exposed to experimental conditions with identical stimuli and standardized procedures produced SET data of such wide variation that some statistical techniques became unusable (Clayson & Frost, 1997).

Strong between-class reliability has created another interesting problem. Langbein (1994) used an established instrument to measure student satisfaction with instruction. The form had 19 questions that formed one factor and resulted in a Cronbach's alpha of 0.99. To investigate what the form measured, a regression utilizing 16 different student, faculty, and situational differences was run that accounted for approximately 12% of the total variance of the evaluations. In other words, an instrument with almost perfect reliability did not account for almost 90% of the total variability in students' responses. This indicates that measurement error is not likely to be the major source of the unexplained variance. Students are responding to something consistently, but it does not appear to be readily apparent what that is, or if, when found, the consistency would be compatible with instructional theory. In other words, the instruments may be suffering from a lack of discriminate validity even though they have a very robust instructor-class reliability. A similar problem was reported by Dodeen (2013) when evaluating a short form of SET. The form showed consistency over time and "acceptable reliability," but it lacked, in this case, content validity.

Inter-Rater Reliability

Inter-item consistency is important to any instrument with multiple items. However, if the purpose of reliability is to serve as an antecedent to validity, it has been argued that any measure of reliability that does not show inter-rater consistency cannot be an adequate precursor to validity (Hayes & Krippendorff, 2007; Krippendorff, 2009; Morley, 2012). If a construct can be understood by an evaluator, and if the construct can be measured with a valid instrument, then any randomly selected evaluator should agree with any other randomly selected evaluator. Krippendorff's Alpha was created to look at the agreement among raters (Krippendorff, 2009, 2011). A high Alpha indicates high agreement, while a low score indicates the raters are responding in a more random fashion. An Alpha of zero would indicate a pure random pattern of responses. Morley (2012) looked at the evaluations of over a thousand classes and found not a single Krippendorff coefficient that exceeded 0.5; about a fourth were negative. Another study looked at different types of reliabilities in a set of SETs. All were found to have high Cronbach Alphas, but almost all had Krippendorff Alphas no different from zero, indicating the differences between students were almost identical to what would be expected by chance. This implies the students did not agree on what they were scaling, or if they did agree, the test items themselves did not allow them to express it (Clayson, 2018). If reliability is seen as respondent consistency rather than class-average consistency, then SET has been shown to have very low and unacceptable levels of reliability.

Summary

1 Reliability is a precursor to validity. However, an instrument can be reliable without being valid.

Challenging the Statistical Reliability 85

2 The evaluations have been found to be consistent over long periods of performance.
3 There is a consensus the evaluation process is remarkably consistent for individual instructors across class averages.
4 Carefully crafted evaluations show high inter-item reliability as measured by traditional statistics, such as Cronbach's Alpha.
5 The consistency of class averages and strong associational relationships between test items does not take into account a surprising amount of inter-rater differences.
6 Newer studies of independent observers of the same instructor have indicated very low SET reliability. Noting this, some have argued that reliability serves as a mixed precursor of SET validity.

References

Al-Eidan, F., Baig, L. A., Magzoub, M., & Omair, A. (2016). Reliability and validity of the faculty evaluation instrument used at King Saud bin Abdulaziz university for health sciences: Results from the haematology course. *Journal of Pakistan Medical Association*, *66*(4), 453–457. Retrieved from www.jpma.org.pk/Pdf Download/7711.pdf

Cashin, W. E. (1995). *Student ratings of teaching: The research revisited* (IDEA Paper No. 32). Publication of the Center for Faculty Evaluation & Development, Division of continuing Education, Kansas State University. Retrieved from https://files.eric.ed.gov/fulltext/ED402338.pdf

Churchill, G. A., & Brown, T. J. (2004). *Basic Marketing Research* (5th ed.). Mason, OH: South-Western.

Clayson, D. E. (2018). Student evaluation of teaching and matters of reliability. *Assessment & Evaluation in Higher Education*, *43*(4), 666–681. https://doi.org/10.1080/02602938.2017.1393495

Clayson, D. E., & Frost, T. F. (1997). An empirical study of the influence of performance and grades on students' evaluation of instruction. *Psychological Reports*, *81*, 507–512. https://doi.org/10.2466/pr0.1997.81.2.507

Dodeen, H. (2013). Validity, reliability, and potential bias of short forms of students' evaluation of teaching: The case of UAE University. *Educational Assessment*, *18*(4), 235–250. https://doi.org/10.1080/10627197.2013.846670

Feldman, K. A. (1983). The seniority and instructional experience of college teachers as related to the evaluations they receive from their students. *Research in Higher Education*, *5*, 243–288. https://doi.org/10.1007/BF00992080

Follman, J. (1984, September). Pedagogue . . . paragon and pariah . . . 20% of the time: Implications for teacher merit pay. *American Psychologist*, 1069–1070. https://doi.org/10.1037/0003-066X.39.9.1069

Gillmore, G. M., Kane, M. T., & Naccarato, R. W. (1978). The generalization of student ratings of instruction: Estimation of the teacher and course components. *Journal of Educational Measurement*, *15*(1), 1–13. https://doi.org/10.1111/j.1745-3984.1978.tb00051.x

Hayes, A. F., & Krippendorff, K. (2007). Answering the call for a standard reliability measure for coding data. *Communication Methods and Measures*, *1*(1), 77–89. https://doi.org/10.1080/19312450709336664

Krippendorff, K. (2009). Testing the reliability of central analysis data: What is involved and why. In K. H. Krippendorff & M. A. Bock (Eds.), *The content analysis reader*. Thousand Oaks, CA: Sage Publication.

Krippendorff, K. (2011). Agreement and information in the reliability of coding. *Communication Methods and Measures*, *5*(2), 93–112. https://doi.org/10.1080/19312458.2011.568376

Langbein, L. I. (1994, September). The validity of student evaluations of teaching. *PS: Political Science in Institutional Politics*, 545–552. https://doi.org/10.2307/420225

Marsh, H. W., & Hocevar, D. (1991). Students' evaluation of teaching effectiveness: The stability of mean rating of the same teachers over a 13-year period. *Teaching & Teaching Education*, *7*(4), 303–314. https://doi.org/10.1016/0742-051X(91)90001-6

Marsh, H. W., & Roche, L. A. (1997). Making students' evaluations of teaching effectiveness effective. *American Psychologist*, *52*(11), 1187–1197. https://doi.org/10.1037/0003-066X.52.11.1187

Morley, D. D. (2012). Claims about the reliability of student evaluations of instruction: The ecological fallacy rides again. *Studies in Educational Evaluation*, *38*, 15–20. https://doi.org/10.1016/j.stueduc.2012.01.001

Overall, J. U., & Marsh, H. W. (1980). Students' evaluations of instruction: A longitudinal study of their stability. *Journal of Educational Psychology*, *72*, 321–325. https://doi.org/10.1037/0022-0663.72.3.321

Sixbury, G. R., & Cashin, W. E. (1995). *Descriptions of database for the IDEA diagnostic form* (IDEA Technical Report No. 9). Publication of the Center for Faculty Evaluation & Development, Division of Continuing Education, Kansas State University.

Zhao, J., & Gallant, D. J. (2012). Student evaluation of instruction in higher education: Exploring issues of validity and reliability. *Assessment & Evaluation in Higher Education*, *37*(2), 227–235. https://doi.org/10.1080/02602938.2010.523819

10 Traditional Validity and SET

Do the Standard Definitions of Validity Apply to the Evaluations?

Li Hui approached his dean with a concern. He is thought of as the best quantitative analyst in the college and was asked to sit in on a blue-ribbon panel charged with updating the university's SET procedure. "The panel is going to recommend we keep the current form. I think it is a mistake. I am convinced that if we are taken to court, we will not be able to defend the validity of the current instrument. We need to replace it . . . even if the University does not." The dean shakes his head. "No," he says, "we will not change our usage of the evaluation." "But we don't know what it measures," replies Li Hui. "I don't care," the dean says with emphasis. "I am required to evaluate my faculty. The present instrument is authorized to do that. It fulfills its function. If you have something better, let me see it."

Most would agree an instrument that is used to make so many important decisions should be measuring something relevant to those decisions in a valid manner. However, validity of an instrument is goal dependent, and not everyone needs to agree on what those goals may be. An instructor, for example, might see SET as a way to improve teaching or student learning, while an administrator may suggest it doesn't matter what specific details are measured as long as the demand for assessment is complied with appropriately. Seldom is anyone this unidimensional when it comes to the SET procedure, but it again raises the most important questions that can be asked of the evaluations. What do they actually measure, and can the instruments validly measure it? These questions are difficult to answer. There are a number of ways validity can be assessed, and the issue has not been definitely resolved.

Types of Validity

As previously noted, SET instruments are typically employed to measure a hypothetical construct: i.e., "good" and/or "effective" teaching. Unless users of SET want to fall into the tautological trap of suggesting "good" teaching is whatever the instrument says it is, the evaluations must be shown to exhibit a valid relationship with the construct it attempts to measure. Since hypothetical constructs generally have no form or dimension that can be objectively measured, a number of different associations must be established. This raises the possibility that an instrument may be valid in certain ways and simultaneously invalid in others. This has been the general findings with SET (Greenwald, 1997).

Face Validity

Face validity exists when an instrument appears to be measuring what the respondent thinks it should be measuring. It is related to the respondent's experience with the instrument. Since SET instruments are created and sanctioned by the institution, ask questions generally associated with instruction, and are administrated in formalized manners, it would be assumed that SET has face validity (Burdsal & Barbo, 1986).

Content Validity

Content validity is said to exist if the questions on an instrument can be logically said to cover the domain of the construct the instrument is intended to measure. Since most institutions do not have a clearly defined notion of what they are attempting to measure (Onwuegbuzie, Daniel, & Collins, 2009; Ory & Ryan, 2001), the content validity of SET is suspect. This is compounded by a disagreement that sometimes arises between the institution and students about the nature of the construct. It has been pointed out that in many institutions there is a gap between what developers of SET consider to be characteristics of effective instructors and what students believe (Lauer, 2012; Onwuegbuzie et al., 2009). Chonko (2004), for example, listed six characteristics students expect from a good instructor, but students did not put the same importance on these aspects of instruction as did the professors. The proportion of students who thought enthusiasm was an important characteristic was more than twice that of instructors (38% of students vs. 18% of instructors). The same discrepancy was found in other research for communication skills (34% vs. 20%) and caring-empathy (24% vs. 14%) (Kelley, Conant, & Smart, 1991). These issues have led to claims that there is a disconnect between what students and faculty believe are important characteristics of good instruction (Spooren, Brockx, & Mortelmans, 2013). For example, when instructor characteristics are factor analyzed, the first factor has been found to be related to caring and being supportive rather than being professionally competent (Keeley, Smith, & Buskist, 2006). When Clayson and Haley (2011) asked students, "Do you think the questions on the evaluation allow you to express what you really want to say on the evaluations?" 45% of the students said "no." One source began their own investigation by stating, "Researchers do not know if what they are asking students to evaluate has any relative importance to them when assessing their course or instructor" (Hills, Naegle, & Bartkus, 2009, p. 297). One random survey of evaluations claimed that the majority of questions on the forms were so ambiguous that it was difficult to determine what they were asking. In addition, about 90% of the questions were not even associated with actual classroom teaching behavior (Lazos, 2012; Tagamori & Bishop, 1995). As Onwuegbuzie et al. (2007) stated, research results have cast "serious doubt" on the content validity of the instruments.

As discussed in a previous chapter, some have attempted to skirt the definitional issue by making "learning" the end result of "effective" teaching, but even here, definitions of "learning" can vary widely (Clayson, 2009) and may be contradictory. The definitional problem is so common and so difficult to resolve, some critics have suggested it is purposeful. Moore and Flinn (2009) state, "many people do not want a definitive measurement of student learning, and they will fight long and hard to prevent one from coming into being" (p. 102).

Concurrent and Predictive Validity

SET results are related to other measures of teaching effectiveness and seem to be predictive of measures made by former students, self-reports, and even of trained observers (Feldman, 1989b; Howard, Conway, & Maxwell, 1985; Marsh & Dunkin, 1992; Onwuegbuzie et al., 2009). In other words, the evaluations appear to have an acceptable level of both concurrent and predictive validity.

Problems arise with concurrent and predictive validity if the comparison instruments are biased. The ratings on RateMyProfessors.com can serve as an example. They have been found to be highly related to SET results from the same institutions (Brown, Baillie, & Fraser, 2009; Coladarci & Kornfield, 2007; Sanders, Walia, Potter, & Linna, 2011), but the associations are also related to relatively irrelevant measures (Clayson, 2014), and might not be adequate in making direct comparisons (Murray & Zdravkovic, 2016).

Construct Validity: Convergent, Discriminant, and Divergent

As indicated by the findings of concurrent validity, SET appears to have convergent validity in that the results are related to other measures that could logically be assumed to be associated with the domain of "effective teaching." Convergent validity is not sufficient, however, to establish construct validity. As an extreme example, a measure that was correlated with *everything* would, by default, be related to the characteristics of any randomly selected construct. Consequently, a demonstration of construct validity must also show that the instrument is not associated with aspects of unrelated constructs (divergent validity), and that it shows differences between the construct of interest and other constructs that are distinct but similar (discriminant validity). While some researchers maintain the evaluations have both convergent and discriminant validity under certain conditions (Marsh, Dicke, & Pfeiffer, 2019), others disagree. After reviewing the results of a study of over 2,000 business students using path analysis, Marks (2000, p. 117) concluded. "student evaluations lack discriminant validity. No matter how reliable the measures, student evaluations are no more than perceptions and impressions." Greenwald (1997) had come to the same conclusion earlier, pointing out that while evaluations of instructors have convergent validity, they are lacking in discriminant validity. More recent critics suggest that the evaluations also lack divergent validity (Langbein, 2008; Onwuegbuzie et al., 2009; Sproule, 2002). In other words, SET is correlated with attributes a concept of "good" teaching would be expected to include, but they are also correlated with numerous attributes with which they shouldn't be related. This is exemplified, and is complicated by, the halo effect (Darby, 2007; Keeley, English, Irons, & Henslee, 2013; Orsini, 1988; Shevlin, Banyard, Davies, & Griffiths, 2000).

Teaching is a complex activity with multidimensional implications (Feldman, 1977, 1989a; Marsh, 2007; Marsh & Roche, 1999). Convergent validity and discriminant and divergent invalidity would be expected if the evaluations were effectively measuring one, or a few, of the dimensions deemed relevant to teaching, but not all. Some researchers have suggested SET does indeed produce a single overriding dimension that could be characterized as a "likability" scale (Delucchi & Pelowski, 2000; Clayson & Haley, 1990; Feistauer & Richter, 2018; Marks, 2000; Tang & Tang, 1987). Sproule (2002) pessimistically asserts the problems with construct validity cannot be remedied in a SET system because the model utilized is "underdetermined" in at least two ways: 1) SET does not provide a unique or an unequivocal explanation of a body of data, and 2) multiple models or theories of SET, even if contradictory, can be seen as equally plausible, given the data from SET.

Nomological Validity

Nomological validity is the degree to which a construct behaves as it should within a system (network) of related constructs. This network would include the theoretical framework for what one is attempting to measure, an empirical framework for how it is to be measured, and specification of the linkages among and between these two frameworks (Cronbach & Meehl, 1955). Several attempts have been made in business education to investigate such a network (Clayson & Haley, 1990; Marks, 2000; Paswan & Young, 2002). Clayson and Haley's (1990) study is an early attempt. Students were asked to describe their "best instructor." This data was then utilized to identify underlying factors that were then linked to an actual SET instrument utilizing structural modeling techniques. It was found that a factor most closely representing faculty personality had almost double the influence on the instrument of any other factor. They concluded that the evaluations created what could most accurately be described as a "likability" scale. As shown in this example, attempts to establish validity have encountered a fundamental problem. They attempt to establish a network from students' perceptions of teaching, essentially matching one set of perceptions against another. This would be appropriate if SET was assumed to be a measure of student perceptions without regard to a preexisting and independent, objective construct. At best, these finding can demonstrate SET instruments are compatible with student perceptions. Again, the question arises, what is "good" or "effective" teaching? Predictably, instead of finding a logical nomological network, the research reaffirms SET lacks validity if a standard of teaching excellence is not consistently present in student cognitive structures and perceptions.

Utilitarian Validity

An instrument could hypothetically be useful as a tool to achieve an end, irrespective of any validity to related theoretical constructs. For example, a politician may get elected by making claims about himself that cannot be validated, but which, nevertheless, allow him to achieve office. There are real and compelling reasons why SET is universally utilized for utilitarian purposes. 1) It provides a method of providing feedback about the quality of instruction, which is being increasingly demanded by accreditation and funding bodies. 2) It simplifies administrative decision-making. 3) It involves the student in a customer-like relationship with the institution and with its instructors. 4) It is believed by many administrators that the instruments are useful in identifying the very best and the very worst instructors. SET appears to have good utilitarian validity in an administrative context (Becker, 2000).

Problems With Utilitarian Validity

Since the use of the evaluations is almost universal, and utilitarian validity is seldom addressed, the issue warrants further discussion. Like other standards of validity, utilitarian usage could also result in contradictory findings. If SET is to be utilized as an evaluation tool, then we would be justified in asking if the measures are of value in achieving some utilitarian goal, and if that goal is valid to education (Clayson, 2008). In pragmatic terms, do the total positive effects created by the utilization of SET in the institutional and educational process outweigh the total negative effect of the evaluations?

The question suggests a number of issues:

Does SET Have the Potential of Changing the Fundamental Structure of Higher Education?

There have been several lines of thought on this issue. SET was originally created to improve the quality of education, and defenders of the process would generally agree this has been accomplished. Critics, however, maintain that SET has negatively impacted higher education. One claim suggests the widespread use of the evaluations damage the proper relationship between students and faculty (Stake, 1997). Professors are generally considered to be experts in their fields of study. The SET process implies, at least in part, that students are in a position of evaluating the content of the expert. This has the potential of lowering the perception of the instructor. The author once took an advanced statistical course from two internationally known experts. Even though the students had PhDs or other terminal degrees, no one expected that we, as students, would have the expertise to evaluate the content of this class, and no evaluation was offered to us. Gray and Bermann (2003) maintained the SET procedure demeans faculty. They noted instructors are forbidden to touch the evaluation sheets after they are completed. "This procedure," they claim, "tells the students that the teacher is more than likely to be a cheat and a sneak, who will cook the books if given a chance" (p. 56).

The SET system could also restrict innovation and individuality. While it is true carefully selected questions and large forms will create multidimensional scales, it is also true that without careful manipulation, the evaluations have a tendency to form one or two dimensions, irrespective of what is asked (Greenwald & Gillmore, 1997; Langbein, 1994). If SET is a valid method of assessing instruction, collapsing scales could suggest that there is only one correct way to teach. In addition, the argument has been made that the widespread utilization of SET has harmonized the faculty (Chisholm, 1977).

There is a Temptation to Utilize the Evaluations Unfairly

As an example, many institutions use the same SET instrument over large discipline domains, even though research shows student evaluations differ by academic discipline (Narayanan, Sawaya, & Johnson, 2014). More objective-oriented classes, such as math and science, receive lower evaluations than do more subjectively graded subjects, such as English, history, and psychology (Uttl & Smibert, 2017). Hoyt and Lee (2002) found differences in almost all discipline areas. The authors state, "Results differ significantly across disciplines, and some of these differences are substantial" (p. 55). If evaluations are valid, then these studies suggest that the best teachers are in areas such as English literature, general education, art, and communications, while the worst teachers are in disciplines such as chemistry, physics, mathematics, economics, and accounting. Beran and Violato (2006) also found substantial discipline differences, but minimized these by concluding, "our results suggest that students may give high ratings to instructors they consider to be effective. In other words, student ratings may be mostly influenced by the behavior of the instructors themselves" (p. 600). Others have taken a casual approach to these differences by simply noting, without explanation, that they exist (Benton & Cashin, 2014; Neumann, 2001).

It seems illogical to this writer that "good" or "effective" teachers concentrate into specific disciplines. Nevertheless, as claimed by Uttl and Smibert (2017), instructors in more objectively defined areas are "far less likely" to receive teaching awards and other benefits of positive evaluations if they are based on summative SET ratings.

The Interpretation of SET Findings has Ontological Inconsistencies With the Design and Constraints of the Evaluations

Assumptions of what the instruments are capable of measuring are seldom questioned in application. There are preexisting assumptions of who and what SET is measuring, which can influence decisions made with the instruments.

Who are the instruments measuring? First, what assumptions are made about the students making the assessment, and second, are the evaluations measuring instructors, instruction, or the students themselves?

With almost no discussion, the current use of SET is consistent with the assumption that students are customers. However, students can also be seen as partners or products of the educational experience (Clayson & Haley, 2005). If a student is a partner, then the SET process is inadequate and limited to only their experience in the classroom. If students are seen as products, then the students should be evaluated, and not instructors. As Hocutt (1987, p. 59) stated, "If we truly want to discover which teachers make a positive and lasting difference, we will not poll pupils; we will examine them." If, on the other hand, students are seen as customers, then their satisfaction with the "service" provider is of prime importance, which appears to be the paradigm assumed by a number of researchers (Berk, 2013; Hativa, 2014; Wright, 2006).

The utilitarian use of SET typically assumes the students are assessing the act of teaching rather than the outcome of instruction. This difference is typically ignored, even though it creates interpretational problems. A related assumption is the evaluations assess instructors rather than classes. An example could be an instructor who teaches multi-sections of the same class. Entire classes have what experienced teachers will sometime identify as a personality. In other words, classes are different, somewhat like individuals are different, and they have a tendency to give different evaluations. Recognizing this difference, researchers and administrators would be less likely to say something to the effect that the instructor taught one section well, or taught one better than the other.

What is SET measuring? Preexisting assumptions of what SET is measuring can influence research methodologies and conclusions. Most assumptions fall into one of four categories.

1   The instruments are measuring "good" or "effective" teaching. Compiling reviewers of SET research, like William Cashin (see Cashin, 1995; Benton & Cashin, 2014; Sixbury & Cashin, 1995), explain SET problems in terms of controls and corrections of the evaluation process compatible with this position. In this view, an administrator would see an apparent gender bias as an error that a possible re-editing of the form would correct.
2   It is not known what the instruments are actually measuring. Bias, inconsistences, and other problems are seen as indicators or reflections of what that core may be. An administrator with this assumption would see a gender bias as evidence that the SET is not a valid measure of teaching.
3   The instruments are measuring student perceptions (Marks, 2000). In this view, perceptions are important, especially if student satisfaction is seen as an essential component of the instructional process. If administrators find perceptions, like gender preference, problematic, they would assume students' perception are in need of correction (Machina, 1987).
4   The SET process fulfills an institutional requirement. In this orientation, SET has a utilitarian value irrespective of anything it may or may

not measure. Relevant research looks primarily at ways to facilitate the process.

The Utilitarian Validity of SET Could Be Compromised by Potential Civil Rights and Diversity Issues

The utilitarian validity of SET would be challenged if it propagated civil and diversity inequalities. As stated by Edmundson (1997), "A controversial teacher can send students hurrying to the deans and counselors, claiming to have been offended" (p. 45). A writer from a law school echoed these concerns, relating them to race and gender, "Few studies engage the eloquent critiques that individual minority professors have raised, and schools do not seem to have examined their practices in response to these concerns" (Merritt, 2007, p. 5). Research at a southern university in the United States found that students rated both the teacher and the course lower for black instructors than for white instructors (Smith & Hawkins, 2011). In addition, data from the 25 highest-ranked liberal arts colleges in America on RateMyProfessors.com showed black and Asian instructors were evaluated more negatively than white instructors. Black males were evaluated more negatively than any other racial and gender combination (Reid, 2010). Online evidence could be questioned, except the average quality ratings from this site have been found to be highly related to SET scores from the same institutions (Coladarci & Kornfield, 2007; Sanders et al., 2011). Further, the site is used by some college-rating services to rank colleges and universities (Howard, 2013). Sinclair and Kunda (2000) reviewed literature that showed people will judge a member of a stigmatized group who evaluates them negatively to be less competent than they would judge a person from a non-stigmatized group. They hypothesized that students would evaluate a female instructor who gave a low grade more negatively than a male instructor who did the same. It is not surprising that international and cultural differences have also been found relating to gender issues in SET (Al-Issa & Sulieman, 2007).

As indicated earlier, about 20% of instructors are rated by students (in the same class) as the best or the worst teachers they have *ever* had (Follman, 1984). The instructors who consistently fall into this 20% are likely to be different in some way; particularly in personality and teaching styles, but in some instances, even in geographical, social class, or racial backgrounds. What happens to instructors who present controversial ideas, or who espouse opinions or ideologies that students may see as incorrect or threatening at any particular moment in time? What if students decide only white males, or black females, are good instructors, and if the evaluations are used uncritically, who is justified, and on what basis, in telling the students they are wrong? To suggest students will separate and remove their biases unrelated to instruction on some anonymous and subjective measure of instructional proficiency is extraordinarily naïve.

Utilizing SET for Utilitarian Reasons May Affect Instructor Morale

Faculty may wonder about the value of the evaluations and the purpose for which they are used when the primary function appears to be a compliance with bureaucratic dictates (Kogan, Schoenfeld-Tacher, & Hellyer, 2010). Penny and Coe (2004) note, "A frequent complaint from teachers . . . is that the principal purpose for collecting student ratings is not necessarily teaching improvement but, rather, use of the data as a politically expedient performance measure for quality monitoring" (p. 215).

SET Creates and Reinforces a Bureaucratic System

Bureaucracies emphasize process over outcomes, or, as pointed out by Howard (2019), "By forcing us to focus on the formal criteria instead of ultimate goals, it effectively shuts the door on the deep well of human skill, experience, and values" (p. 48). The result has been summed up in something called Campbell's Law, "The more any quantitative social indicator is used for social decision-making, the more subject it will be to corruption pressures and the more apt it will be to distort and corrupt the social processes it is intended to monitor" (Campbell, 1979; Sidorkin, 2016, p. 321).

Summary

1 The validity of the evaluation process has been hard to ascertain and is fundamentally complicated by the lack of standardized definitions.
2 Advocates, such as Herbert Marsh, defend the evaluations and their usefulness, and generally interpret findings as being positive on issues of validity.
3 The evaluations are generally seen as having face and convergent validity. They have questionable content validity, and have been consistently criticized for lacking discriminant and divergent validity. Research on predictive validity has shown mixed results, depending to a large extent on what the instrument is utilized to predict.
4 Nomologically, what the evaluations seem to measure most consistently is a perception of what the students liked and disliked.

5 Utilitarian validity is mixed. On one hand, SET fulfills a genuine and valuable function. However, utilitarian applications can also be seen as harming legitimate pedagogic goals.

References

Al-Issa, A., & Sulieman, H. (2007). Student evaluations of teaching: Perceptions and biasing factors. *Quality Assurance in Education, 15*(3), 302–317. https://doi.org/10.1108/09684880710773183

Becker, W. (2000). Teaching economics in the 21th century. *Journal of Economic Perspectives, 14*(1), 109–119. https://doi.org/10.1257/jep.14.1.109

Benton, S. L., & Cashin, W. E. (2014). *Student ratings of teaching: A summary of research and literature* (IDEA PAPER No. 50). Manhattan, KS: The IDEA Center. Retrieved from http://citeseerx.ist.psu.edu/viewdoc/download?doi=10.1.1.388.8561&rep=rep1&type=pdf

Beran, T., & Violato, C. (2006). Ratings of university teacher instruction: How much do student and course characteristics really matter? *Assessment & Evaluation in Higher Education, 30*(6), 593–601. https://doi.org/10.1080/02602930500260688

Berk, R. A. (2013). *Top 10 flashpoints in student ratings and the evaluation of teaching*. Sterling VA: Stylus.

Brown, M. J., Baillie, M., & Fraser, S. (2009). Rating RateMyProfessors.com: A comparison of online and official student evaluation of teaching. *College Teaching, 57*(2), 89–92. https://doi.org/10.3200/CTCH.57.2.89-92

Burdsal, C. A., & Barbo, J. W. (1986). Measuring students' perceptions of teaching: Dimensions of evaluation. *Educational & Psychological Measurement, 46*(1), 63–79. https://doi.org/10.1177/0013164486461006

Campbell, D. T. (1979). Assessing the impact of planned social change. *Evaluation and Program Planning, 2*(1), 67–90. https://doi.org/10.1016/0149-7189(79)90048-X

Cashin, W. E. (1995). *Student ratings of teaching: The research revisited* (IDEA Paper No. 32). Publication of the Center for Faculty Evaluation & Development, Division of continuing Education, Kansas State University. Retrieved from https://files.eric.ed.gov/fulltext/ED402338.pdf

Chisholm, M. G. (1977). Student evaluation: The red herring of the decade. *Journal of Chemical Education, 54*(1), 22–23. Retrieved from https://pubs.acs.org/doi/pdf/10.1021/ed054p22

Chonko, L. B. (2004). If it walks like a duck . . .: Concerns about quackery in marketing education. *Journal of Marketing Education, 26*, 4–16. https://doi.org/10.1177/0273475303257763

Clayson, D. E. (2008). A new concept of validity: Evaluation of teaching, and the production of loincloths. In R. A. Lupton & B. L. Gross (Eds.), *Reaching new heights in marketing education: Marketing educators' association 2008 conference proceedings* (pp. 7–11). Salt Lake City. Retrieved from www.marketingeducators.org/proceedings

Clayson, D. E. (2009). Student evaluation of teaching: Are they related to what students learn? A meta-analysis and review of the literature. *Journal of Marketing Education, 31*(1), 16–30. https://doi.org/10.1177/0273475308324086

Clayson, D. E. (2014). What does RateMyProfessor.com actually rate. *Assessment & Evaluation in Higher Education, 39*(3), 1–21. https://doi.org/10.1080/02602938.2013.861384

Clayson, D. E., & Haley, D. A. (1990, Fall). Student evaluations in marketing: What is actually being measured? *Journal of Marketing Education, 12,* 9–17. https://doi.org/10.1177/027347539001200302

Clayson, D. E., & Haley, D. A. (2005). Marketing models in education: Students as customers, products, or partners. *Marketing Education Review, 15*(1), 1–10. https://doi.org/10.1080/10528008.2005.11488884

Clayson, D. E., & Haley, D. A. (2011). Are students telling us the truth? A critical look at the student evaluation of teaching. *Marketing Education Review, 21*(2), 103–114. https://doi.org/10.2753/MER1052-8008210201

Coladarci, T., & Kornfield, I. (2007). RateMyProfessors.com versus formal in-class student evaluations of teaching. *Practical Assessment, Research & Evaluation, 12*(6). Retrieved from http://pareonline.net/getvn.asp?v=12&n6

Cronbach, L., & Meehl, P. (1955). Construct validity in psychological tests. *Psychological Bulletin, 52*(4), 281–302. https://doi.org/10.1037/h0040957

Darby, J. A. (2007). Are course evaluations subject to a halo effect? *Research in Higher Education, 77,* 46–55. https://doi.org/10.7227/RIE.77.4

Delucchi, M., & Pelowski, S. (2000). Liking or learning? The effect of instructor likability and student perceptions of learning on overall ratings of teaching ability. *Radical Pedagogy, 2*(2). Retrieved from http://radicalpedagogy.icaap.org/content/issue2_2/delpel.html

Edmundson, M. (1997, September). On the uses of a liberal education: Essay I. As lite entertainment for bored college students. *Harper's Magazine,* 39–49. Retrieved from rchive.harpers.org/1997/09/pdf/HarpersMagazine-1997–09–0074348.pdf?AWSAccessKeyId=AKIAJXATU3VRJAAA66RA&Expires=1415081482&Signature=hDuDYQW5y81lixHWaPtRklciVZM%3D

Feistauer, D., & Richter, T. (2018). Validity of students' evaluations of teaching: Biasing effects of likability and prior subject interest. *Educational Evaluation, 59,* 168–178. https://doi.org/10.1016/j.stueduc.2018.07.009

Feldman, K. A. (1977). Consistency and variability among college students in rating their teachers and courses: A review and analysis. *Research in Higher Education, 6*(3), 223–274. https://doi.org/10.1007/BF00991288

Feldman, K. A. (1989a). The association between student ratings of specific instructional dimensions and student achievement: Refining and extending the synthesis of data from multisection validity studies. *Research in Higher Education, 30,* 583–645. https://doi.org/10.1007/BF00992392

Feldman, K. A. (1989b). Instructional effectiveness of college teachers as judged by teachers themselves, current and former students, colleagues, administrators, and external observers. *Research in Higher Education, 30,* 137–194. https://doi.org/10.1007/BF00992716

Follman, J. (1984, September). Pedagogue . . . paragon and pariah . . . 20% of the time: Implications for teacher merit pay. *American Psychologist,* 1069–1070. https://doi.org/10.1037/0003-066X.39.9.1069

Gray, M., & Bermann, B. R. (2003, September–October). Student teaching evaluations: Inaccurate, demeaning, misused. *Academe*, 44–46. Retrieved from http://web.utk.edu/~senate/TeachingEvaluations.pdf

Greenwald, A. G. (1997). Validity concerns and usefulness of student ratings of instruction. *American Psychologist*, *52*(11), 1182–1186. https://doi.org/10.1037/0003-066X.52.11.1182

Greenwald, A. G., & Gillmore, G. M. (1997). Grading leniency is a removable contaminant of student ratings. *American Psychologist*, *52*(11), 1209–1217. https://doi.org/10.1037/0003-066X.52.11.1209

Hativa, N. (2014). *Student rating of instruction: Recognizing efective teacher* (2nd ed.). eBook: Oron Publications.

Hills, S. B., Naegle, N., & Bartkus, K. R. (2009, May–June). How important are items on a student evaluation? A study of item salience. *Journal of Education for Business*, 297–303. https://doi.org/10.3200/JOEB.84.5.297-303

Hocutt, M. (1987, Winter). Degrading student evaluations: What's wrong with student polls of teaching. *Academic Questions*, 55–64. Retrieved from https://www.researchgate.net/profile/Max_Hocutt/publication/248140619_Degrading_student_evaluations_What's_wrong_with_student_polls_of_teaching/links/574a4a9408ae5bf2e63f1d9a.pdf

Howard, C. (2013, July 24). Ranking America's top colleges 2013. *Forbes*. Retrieved from www.forbes.com/sites/carolinehoward/2013/07/24/ranking-americas-top-colleges-2013

Howard, G. S., Conway, C. G., & Maxwell, S. E. (1985). Construct validity of measures of college teaching effectiveness. *Journal of Educational Psychology*, *77*, 187–196. https://doi.org/10.1037/0022-0663.77.2.187

Howard, P. K. (2019). *Try common sense*. New York: W. W. Norton & Company.

Hoyt, D. P., & Lee, E. (2002). *Teaching styles and learning outcomes* (IDEA Research Report #4). The IDEA Center. Retrieved from https://files.eric.ed.gov/fulltext/ED472498.pdf

Keeley, J. W., English, T., Irons, J., & Henslee, A. M. (2013). Investigating halo and ceiling effects in student evaluations of instruction. *Educational and Psychological Measurement*, *73*(3), 440–457. https://doi.org/10.1177/0013164412475300

Keeley, J. W., Smith, D., & Buskist, W. (2006). The teacher behaviors checklist: Factor analysis of its utility for evaluating teaching. *Teaching of Psychology*, *33*(2), 84–91. https://doi.org/10.1207/s15328023top3302_1

Kelley, C. A., Conant, J. S., & Smart, D. T. (1991). Master teaching revisited: Pursuing excellence from the students' perspective. *Journal of Marketing Education*, *13*, 1–10. https://doi.org/10.1177/027347539101300202

Kogan, L. R., Schoenfeld-Tacher, R., & Hellyer, P. W. (2010). Student evaluations of teaching: Perceptions of faculty based on gender, position, and rank. *Teaching in Higher Education*, *15*(6), 623–636. https://doi.org/10.1080/13562517.2010.491911

Langbein, L. I. (1994, September). The validity of student evaluations of teaching. *PS: Political Science in Institutional Politics*, 545–552. https://doi.org/10.2307/420225

Langbein, L. I. (2008). Management by results: Student evaluation of faculty teaching and the mis-measurement of performance. *Economics of Education Review*, *27*, 417–428. https://doi.org/10.1016/j.econedurev.2006.12.003

Lauer, C. (2012). A comparison of faculty and student perspectives on course evaluation. *To Improve the Academy*, *31*(1), 194–211. https://doi.org/10.1002/j.2334-4822.2012.tb00682.x

Lazos, S. R. (2012). Are students teaching evaluations holding back women and minorities? The perils of "Doing" gender and race in the classroom. In G. Gutierrez Muhs, Y. F. Niemann, C. G. Gonzalez, & A. P. Harris (Eds.), *Presumed incompetent: The intersections of race and class for women in Academia*. Utah State University Press, University Press of Colorado. Retrieved from www.jstor.org/stable/j.ctt4cgr3k.19

Machina, K. (1987, May–June). Evaluating student evaluations. *Academe*, 19–22. Retrieved from www.jstor.org/stable/40249936?seq=1

Marks, R. B. (2000). Determinants of student evaluations of global measures of instructor and course value. *Journal of Marketing Education*, *22*(2), 108–119. https://doi.org/10.1177/0273475300222005

Marsh, H. W., Dicke, T., & Pfeiffer, M. (2019). A tale of two quests: The (almost) non-overlapping research literature on students' evaluations of secondary-school and university teachers. *Contemporary Educational Psychology*, *58*, 1–18. https://doi.org/10.1016/j.cedpsych.2019.01.011

Marsh, H. W., & Dunkin, M. (1992). Students' evaluations of university teaching: A multidimensional perspective. In J. C. Smart (Ed.) *Higher education: Handbook of theory and research* (Vol. 8, pp. 143–233). New York: Agathon.

Marsh, H. W., & Roche, L. A. (1999). Reply upon set research. *American Psychologist*, *54*(7), 517–518. https://doi.org/10.1037/0003-066X.54.7.517

Marsh, W. H. (2007). Do university teachers become more effective with experience? A multilevel growth model of students' evaluations of teaching over 13 years. *Journal of Educational Psychology*, *99*(4), 775–790. https://doi.org/10.1037/0022-0663.99.4.775

Merritt, D. J. (2007). *Bias, the brain, and student evaluations of teaching* (Express O Preprint Series, Paper 1939). The Berkeley Electronic Press. Retrieved from http://law.bepress.com/expresso/eps/1939.

Moore, P., & Flinn, R. E. (2009). The limitations of measuring student learning. In R. E. Flinn & D. L. Crumbley (Eds.), *Measure learning rather than satisfaction in higher education*. Sarasota, FL: American Accounting Association.

Murray, K. B., & Zdravkovic, S. (2016). Does MTV really do a good job of evaluating professors? An empirical test of the internet site RateMyProfessors.com. *Journal of Education for Business*, *91*(3), 138–147. https://doi.org/10.1080/08832323.2016.1140115

Narayanan, A., Sawaya, W. J., & Johnson, M. D. (2014). Analysis of differences in nonteaching factors influencing student evaluation of teaching between engineering and business classrooms. *Decision Sciences Journal of Innovative Education*, *12*(3), 233–265. https://doi.org/10.1111/dsji.12035

Neumann, R. (2001). Disciplinary differences and university teaching. *Studies in Higher Education*, *26*(2), 135–146. https://doi.org/10.1080/03075070120052071

Onwuegbuzie, A. J., Daniel, L. G., & Collins, K. M. T. (2009). A meta-validation model for assessing the score-validity of student teaching evaluations. *Quality & Quantity*, *43*, 197–209. https://doi.org/10.1007/s11135-007-9112-4

Onwuegbuzie, A. J., Witcher, A. E., Collins, K. M. T., Filer, J. D., Wiedmaier, C. D., & Moore, C. W. (2007). Characteristics of effective college teachers: A validity study of a teaching evaluation form using a mixed-methods analysis. *American Educational Research Journal*, *44*(1), 113–160. https://doi.org/10.3102/0002831206298169

Orsini, J. L. (1988, Summer). Halo effects in student evaluations of faculty: A case application. *Journal of Marketing Education*, *10*, 38–45. https://doi.org/10.1177/027347538801000208

Ory, J. C., & Ryan, K. (2001). How do student ratings measure up to a new validity framework? *New Directions in Institutional Research*, *109*, 27–44. https://doi.org/10.1002/ir.2

Paswan, A. K., & Young, J. A. (2002). Student evaluation of instructors: A nomological investigation using structural modeling. *Journal of Marketing Education*, *24*, 193–202. https://doi.org/10.1177/0273475302238042

Penny, A. R., & Coe, R. (2004). Effectiveness of consultation on student ratings feedback: Meta-analysis. *Review of Educational Research*, *74*(2), 215–253. https://doi.org/10.3102/00346543074002215

Reid, L. D. (2010). The role of perceived race and gender in the evaluation of college teaching on RateMyProfessors.com. *Journal of Diversity in Higher Education*, *3*(3), 137–152. https://doi.org/10.1037/a0019865

Sanders, S., Walia, B., Potter, J., & Linna, K. W. (2011). Do more online instructional ratings lead to better prediction of instructor quality? *Practical Assessment, Research & Evaluation*, *16*(2). Retrieved from http://pareonline.net/pdf/v16n2.pdf.

Shevlin, M., Banyard, P., Davies, M., & Griffiths, M. (2000). The validity of student evaluation of teaching in higher education: Love me, love my lectures? *Assessment & Evaluation in Higher Education*, *25*(4), 397–405. https://doi.org/10.1080/713611436

Sidorkin, A. M. (2016). Campbell's Law and the ethics of immensurability. *Studies in Philosophy and Education*, *35*, 321–332. https://doi.org/10.1007/s11217-015-9482-3

Sinclair, L., & Kunda, Z. (2000). Motivated stereotyping of women: She is fine if she praised me but incompetent if she criticized me. *Personality and Social Psychology Bulletin*, *26*(11), 1329–1342. https://doi.org/10.1177/0146167200263002

Sixbury, G. R., & Cashin, W. E. (1995). *Descriptions of database for the IDEA diagnostic form* (IDEA Technical Report No. 9). Publication of the Center for Faculty Evaluation & Development, Division of Continuing Education, Kansas State University.

Smith, B. P., & Hawkins, B. (2011). Examing student evaluations of black college faculty: Does race matter? *The Journal of Negro Education*, *80*(2), 149–162. Retrieved from www.jstor.org/stable/41341117

Spooren, P., Brockx, B., & Mortelmans, D. (2013). On the validity of student evaluation of teaching: The state of the art. *Review of Educational Research*, *83*(4), 598–642. https://doi.org/10.3102/0034654313496870

Sproule, R. (2002). The under-determination of instructor performance by data from the student evaluation of teaching. *Economics of Education Review*, *21*(3), 287–295. https://doi.org/10.14507/epaa.v8n50.2000

Stake, J. E. (1997). Response to Haskell: Academic freedom. Tenure, and student evaluation of faculty. *Education Policy Archives*, *5*(8). Retrieved from www//epaa.asu.edu/epaa/v5n8.html.

Tagamori, H. T., & Bishop, L. A. (1995). Student evaluation of teaching: Flaws in the instruments. *Thought & Action*, *11*(1), 63–78. https://eric.ed.gov/?id=EJ506864

Tang, T. L., & Tang, T. L. (1987, Spring). A correlation study of students' evaluations of faculty performance and their self-ratings in an instructional setting. *College Student Journal*, *21*, 90–97. https://files.eric.ed.gov/fulltext/ED279981.pdf

Uttl, B., & Smibert, D. (2017). Student evaluations of teaching: Teaching quantitative course can be hazardous to one's career. *PeerJ*, e3299. https://doi.org/10.7717/peerj.3299

Wright, R. E. (2006). Student evaluations of faculty: Concerns raised in the literature, and possible solutions. *College Student Journal*, *40*(2), 417–422. Retrieved from www.questia.com/read/1G1-147389148/student-evaluations-of-faculty-concerns-raised-in

11 Identifying Valid Applications of SET

Are the Evaluations Valid Over Wide Applications?

Palmer, who is serving as the head of a university committee to create a new evaluation instrument, leaned back in his chair and stretched. It was almost midnight and he had been struggling with his summary report all day. The mountain of research his committee had amassed defiantly rejected an easy conclusion, but it was the validity issue that bothered Palmer the most. Yes, the SET process was valid. No, it was not valid. There was little agreement and, even worse, the traditional indices of validity were also inconsistent. Could the evaluations be both valid and invalid at the same time? Perhaps it depended on what the process was engaged to do? "Ouch," he said to himself, "it is going to be a long night."

Palmer's suspicion that there was not a simple answer to the problem of validity is accurate. In fact, the issue goes beyond the traditional theoretical and metric-oriented validity indices. A SET instrument found to be valid for one application does not necessarily ensure validity when the instrument is elsewhere applied.

Validity and Purpose

SET instruments have a number of applications. They could be utilized for: 1) instructional improvement, the so-called *formative function*; 2) evaluation of performance with personnel and managerial implications, the *summative function*; and/or 3) necessary feedback to comply with legislative, administrative, or student demands, or a *utilitarian function*. One question that needs to be addressed in any discussion of validity is the domain in which an instrument may be utilized.

Formative Function: Instructional Improvement

Although the evidence is mixed, the research into the evaluations has generally found the instruments fail the formative function, i.e., improving instruction. Most research has not found sufficient improvement of instruction by using feedback from SET, as measured by the same or similar instruments (Campbell & Bozeman, 2007). In Cohen's (1980) meta-analysis, not only was there no improvement in the majority of factors studied, students whose instructors received midterm feedback did not learn more than students whose instructors did not receive feedback.

Summative Function: Evaluation of Performance

Determining the validity of SET utilized as a summative instrument is difficult. Managers are generally required to evaluate the performance of their workers. This is also true in most academic settings. However, the demand for summative utilization raises a number of validity-related questions. For what purpose should performance be evaluated? Who should evaluate performance? And, fundamentally, what is "performance?" Unless we wish to propagate a tautology (see Pinto & Mansfield, 2010), or assume the instruments have only an administrative utilitarian function, the validity of the SET as a summative agent is dependent upon the answers to these questions.

The summative utilization of SET could be justified if it led to improved instruction. However, as previously noted, the evidence for teaching improvement utilizing the evaluations is weak. Even so, there are a number of legitimate administrative outcomes which would justify summative procedures. For example, SET does provide an insight into student perceptions. Perceptions and levels of satisfaction are important to the administrative system, especially if students are seen as customers. Students, however, can be seen in different ways, and attempting to measure all differences in one instrument increases the probability of obtaining invalid measures because it raises the issue of "diagnostic" validity, or the ability of the instruments to clearly identify any given dimension of instruction as distinct from others (Kember & Leung, 2008).

Summative validity is also dependent on accurate definitions of performance. The validity of using the act of teaching to make summative judgments would depend on the definition of desirable behaviors and the accuracy of student assessors. Both of these are compromised by students' propensity to invoke teacher attributes rather than instructional actions (Moore & Kuol, 2007). Further, many SET instruments contain measures made about areas beyond the instructor's control (Mason, Steagall, & Fabritius, 1995). If, on the other hand, performance is defined in terms of what instruction produces, then students should be the object of assessment, not the instructor (Abrami, d'Apollonia, & Rosenfield, 2007). To be clear, if effective teaching is determined by what it produces (other than happy or unhappy students), then the appropriate measure is student performance, and SET, while remaining a potentially useful tool for formative purposes and research, is not justified as a primary summative agent.

Consider the example of an athletic coach at a modern university. Studies of the characteristics of a good coach include many of the attributes found in good teachers (Becker, 2009). However, the job security and salary of coaches is not determined by the perceptions of their students, but by their performance. They must win games. In this case, the validity of the assessment is assured because the purpose of the evaluation, who should perform it, and the metric of performance are all objectively defined.

All of these suggest, along with statistical issues utilized for assessment, that SET must have clear definitions and exhibit thoughtful application to serve as a valid summative instrument.

Utilitarian Function: Compliance

The utilitarian function of the evaluations is an issue that has been largely ignored in the literature. Yet, it has been said that the evaluations will remain a fixture in modern education far into the future (Benton & Cashin, 2014) because of their "utility in academic decision making" (Linse, 2017). "Utility" is based on what some critics have identified as "administrative purposes" (Trout, 2000). In many cases, administrators are required to utilize some sort of faculty evaluation. The pressure to do so has come from a combination of sources including pedagogic, legislative, and student demands, the resolution of which can be a "deeply political process" (Modell, 2005). Some have claimed that even if outside forces were absent, SET is demanded because it helps legitimize "managerial claims to increasing control over the affairs of the university" (Valsan & Sproule, 2008, p. 940). As one unnamed critic stated, SET exists because of administrative sloth and student crowd control. While this statement is overly dramatic, it does emphasize the reality that SET may have a utilitarian usage for reasons other than those traditionally stated.

Validity and Lack of Definitions

Undergirding our discussion is a foundational problem that has run like a thread through all of this discussion. It is difficult – some would say impossible – to validly measure an undefined construct. No one has given a widely accepted definition of what "performance" is in an educational context, let alone a definition of "good" or "effective" teaching (Bedggood & Donovan, 2012; Germain & Scandura, 2005; Hornstein, 2017; Marsh & Roche, 1997; Moore & Flinn, 2009). This was recognized early in the evaluation literature. Over 40 year ago, Hoyt (1973), who referred to "good" teaching as "teaching effectiveness," stated, "Unless there is agreement on how effectiveness can be judged, it will be impossible to develop dependable guides for improving instruction" (p. 368). Even with the massive amount of research that followed, there is still no definitive definition. Hornstein (2017) states,

> There is . . . no specific evidence of content validity that suggests that the instrument used at many universities measures teaching competence. As a matter of fact, to the current author's knowledge, universities tend not to advocate any clear theory of effective teaching.
> (p. 4 of 8)

Consequently, instruments designed to measure the construct are hampered by definitional and resultant methodological restraints.

Validity and Learning

As outlined previously, one attempt to skirt the definitional problem and establish validity has been the general assumption that students will learn more from a "good" instructor. There is substantial evidence the SET procedure currently does not validate this criterion. This, for many, has been hard to accept (Gravestock & Gregor-Greenleaf, 2008; Hativa, 2014). In the past, some highly respected sources claimed a positive relationship, and compilers seldom questioned those sources. Countering traditional assumptions is difficult, especially when the lack of a learning-evaluation relationship has such dramatic implications for the validity of the SET process.

Validity and Attribution

Irrespective of whatever else they may be, the evaluations can be seen as student perceptions (Marks, 2000; Waters, Kemp, & Pucci, 1988), and perceptions are subjective; being created, modified, and given meaning by an observer. Consequently, it is not obvious who is being rated. This problem will be discussed later in detail. Nevertheless, it is not always evident that students are evaluating either the instructor or the instructor's actual performance. There is, for example, the problem of attribution. Student behaviors, both positive and negative, are projected onto the instructor (Gremler & McCollough, 2002). This behavior led Tang and Tang (1987) to conclude that the evaluations might give a better indication of the student's self-concept than the instructor's actual performance. Grimes, Millea, and Woodriff (2004) found students with an external locus of control gave their instructors lower evaluations than students with an internal orientation. Benz and Blatt (1996) affirmed these attribution effects in an analysis of student comments showing students "satisfied" with their grades described their experiences with "I." Students "dissatisfied" with their grades tended to use "he" or "she." For example, "He never gives good grades." An argument can be made that SET is a measure of the students themselves, and not of instructors.

Validity and Statistical, Measurement, and Scaling Concerns

A major problem dealing with the validity of the instruments is related to the statistical methodology employed when utilizing SET data (Kitto, Williams, & Alderman, 2019). Whenever a question is asked that can be quantified, a scale is assumed by the type of answer given, or the type of answer that *can* be given. The appropriateness of a statistical analysis is dependent upon these scales. A number of sources have commented on this issue (Hornstein, 2017; McCullough & Radson, 2011; Porter, 2011). Furthermore, even though institutions seldom define their terms, or identify or explain what constitutes "good teaching" (Burns, 2011), the evaluations are often summarized by a single score from one question (Madu & Kuei, 1993).

An example can be drawn from the writer's own university. For years, the most important measure on the SET, and the one used to make summary comparisons, was a simple ordinal scale which read, "How would you rate the overall effectiveness of the instructor in this course?" The student was given four options: "Highly Ineffective," "Ineffective," "Effective," and "Highly Effective." Nowhere was "effective" defined, nor was the object described by "effective" defined. To the university's credit, the scales were not averaged. The percent of students responding with "Effective" and "Highly Effective" were added together. This, however, created its own problems. Suppose an instructor had 80% of her students rating her as "Effective" and/or "Highly Effective." There are potentially thousands of combinations which would make her equally "effective" to any other instructor who also received 80% of her scores in the same two categories.

Creating a more sophisticated scale does not solve the problem of validly comparing instructors. Suppose a SET created an interval scale and a cutoff was established to quantify who was an "effective" instructor. Statistically, how could anyone below that value be judged as being "ineffective?" The best that can be done is to establish a probability an instructor is "effective." Even then, before these measures could be used in a summative fashion, we would have to assume that the students enrolled in the class were randomly selected from a group of students who would also populate any class taught by instructors who we might wish to compare. In addition, this example assumes the scale produced by the evaluations would create a normal distribution – a condition obviously unmet with the characteristic skewed distribution and the lack of homoscedasticity of the typical bounded SET scale.

SET skewness creates another issue. If the scales are taken literally, almost everyone is a wonderful teacher. Consequently, administrators who wish to make comparative use of the instruments will typically look at percentile scores. This solution creates an extreme sensitivity to negative outliers, especially in a small class. Success, when percentile ranking is used, depends largely on *not* producing outliers. This may create problems for some instructors, especially those who are nontraditional.

Even the number of points in a scale can have dramatic effects. As noted in a previous chapter, utilizing a ten-point scale rather than a five- or six-point scale can result in substantial differences in ratings if there is a bias present. On a ten-point scale, students are more likely to reserve nine and ten for the very top rating, while being much more liberal with applying a top rating on a shorter scale. In male-dominated academic fields, it was found that men will receive higher evaluations than women on ten-point scales, which largely disappear with six-point scales (Rivera & Tilcsik, 2019). The researchers point out evaluations are not neutral instruments, nor are they neutral in their application (Neath, 1996).

These lines of argument suggest that not only do the students make subjective evaluations based on their own perceptions, but administrative decisions based on the instruments are likely to be subjective as well.

Summary

1 An evaluation instrument that is valid for one purpose may be invalid for another.
2 Determining the validity of SET has been hampered by having no widely accepted definition of what the process is intended to measure.
3 If the purpose of the evaluations is to identify teachers from whom students learn, then recent research indicates that the instruments are invalid. They do not generally discriminate between instructors whose students are learning from those who are not.
4 The validity of the instruments has been compromised by the summative utilization of inappropriate assumptions and statistical analyses.

References

Abrami, P. C., d'Apollonia, S., & Rosenfield, S. (2007). The dimensionality of student ratings of instruction: What we know and what we do not. In R. P. Perry & J. C. Smart (Eds.), *The scholarship of teaching and learning in higher education: An evidence-based perspective* (Section II, pp. 385–456). https://doi.org/10.1007/1-4020-5742-3_10

Becker, A. J. (2009). It's not what they do, it's how they do it: Athlete experiences of great coaching. *International Journal of Sports Science and Coaching, 4*(1), 93–114. https://doi.org/10.1260/1747-9541.4.1.93

Bedggood, R. E., & Donovan, J. D. (2012). University performance evaluations: What are we really measuring? *Studies in Higher Education, 37*(7), 825–842. https://doi.org/10.1080/03075079.2010.549221

Benton, S. L., & Cashin, W. E. (2014). *Student ratings of teaching: A summary of research and literature*. Manhattan, KS: The IDEA Center. Retrieved from http://citeseerx.ist.psu.edu/viewdoc/download?doi=10.1.1.388.8561&rep=rep1&type=pdf

Benz, S., & Blatt, S. J. (1996). Meaning underlying student ratings of faculty. *The Review of Higher Education, 19*(4), 411–433. https://muse.jhu.edu/article/644579/pdf

Burns, M. (2011, September 24). Do principles know good teaching when they see it? *Miller-McCune*. Retrieved from www.psmag.com/education/do-principals-know-good-teaching-when-they-see-it-36417.

Campbell, J. P., & Bozeman, W. C. (2007). The value of student ratings: Perceptions of students, teachers, and administrators. *Community College Journal of Research and Practice, 32*(1), 13–24. https://doi.org/10.1080/10668920600864137

Cohen, P. A. (1980). Effectiveness of student-rating feedback for improving college instruction: A meta-analysis. *Research in Higher Education, 13*(4), 321–341. https://doi.org/10.1007/BF00976252

Germain, M., & Scandura, T. A. (2005). Grade inflation and student individual differences as systematic bias in faculty evaluations. *Journal of Instructional Psychology, 32*(1), 58–67. Retrieved from http://people.uncw.edu/caropresoe/EDN523/523_Spr_07/Grade_Inflation.pdf

Gravestock, P., & Gregor-Greenleaf, E. (2008). *Student course evaluations: Research, models, and trends*. Toronto: Higher Education Quality Council of Ontario. https://doi=10.1.1.627.5590rep=rep1&type=pdf

Gremler, D. D., & McCollough, M. A. (2002). Student satisfaction guarantees: An empirical examination of attitudes, antecedents, and consequences. *Journal of Marketing Education, 24*(2), 150–160. https://doi.org/10.1177/027753024002008

Grimes, P. W., Millea, M., & Woodriff, T. W. (2004). Who's to blame? Locus of control and student evaluation of teaching. *Journal of Economic Education, 35*(2), 129–147. https://doi.org/10.3200/JECE.35.2.129-147

Hativa, N. (2014). *Student rating of instruction: Recognizing efective teacher* (2nd ed.). eBook: Oron Publications.

Hornstein, H. A. (2017). Student evaluations of teaching are an inadequate assessment tool for evaluating faculty performance. *Cogent Education, 4*(1), Article 1304016. https://doi:10.1080/2331186X.2017.1304016.

Hoyt, D. P. (1973). Measurement of instructional effectiveness. *Research in Higher Education*, *1*, 367–378.

Kember, D., & Leung, D. Y. P. (2008). Establishing the validity and reliability of course evaluation questionnaires. *Assessment & Evaluation in Higher Education*, *33*(4), 341–353. https://doi.org/10.1080/02602930701563070

Kitto, K. I., Williams, C., & Alderman, L. (2019). Beyond average: Contemporary statistical techniques for analysing student evaluations of teaching. *Assessment & Evaluation in Higher Education*, *44*(3), 338–360. https://doi.org/10.1080/02602938.2018.1506909

Linse, A. R. (2017). Interpreting and using student ratings data: Guidance for faculty serving as administrators and on evaluation committees. *Studies in Educational Evaluation*, *54*, 94–106. https://doi.org/10.1016/j.stueduc.2016.12.004

Madu, C. N., & Kuei, C. (1993). Dimensions of quality teaching in higher institutions. *Total Quality Management*, *4*(3), 325–338. https://doi.org/10.1080/09544129300000046

Marks, R. B. (2000). Determinants of student evaluations of global measures of instructor and course value. *Journal of Marketing Education*, *22*(2), 108–119. https://doi.org/10.1177/0273475300222005

Marsh, H. W., & Roche, L. A. (1997). Making students' evaluations of teaching effectiveness effective. *American Psychologist*, *52*(11), 1187–1197. https://doi.org/10.1037/0003-066X.52.11.1187

Mason, P., Steagall, J., & Fabritius, M. (1995). Student evaluations of faculty: A new procedure for using aggregate measures. *Economics of Education Review*, *12*, 403–416.

McCullough, B. D., & Radson, D. (2011). Analyzing student evaluations of teaching: Comparing means and proportions. *Evaluation & Research in Education*, *24*(3), 183–202. https://doi.org/10.1080/09500790.2011.603411

Modell, S. (2005). Students as consumers? An institutional field-level analysis of the construction of performance measurement practices. *Accounting, Auditing & Accountability Journal*, *18*(4), 537–563. https://doi.org/10.1108/09513570510609351

Moore, P., & Flinn, R. E. (2009). The limitations of measuring student learning. In R. E. Flinn & D. L. Crumbley (Eds.), *Measure learning rather than satisfaction in higher education*. Sarasota, FL: American Accounting Association.

Moore, S., & Kuol, N. (2007). Retrospective insights on teaching: Exploring teaching excellence through the eyes of the alumni. *Journal of Further and Higher Education*, *31*(2), 133–163. https://doi.org/10.1080/03098770701267598

Neath, I. (1996). How to improve your teaching evaluations without improving your teaching. *Psychological Reports*, *78*, 1363–1372. https://doi.org/10.2466/pr0.1996.78.3c.1363

Pinto, M. B., & Mansfield, P. M. (2010). Thought processes college students use when evaluating faculty: A qualitative study. *American Journal of Business Education (AJBE)*, *3*(3), 55–62. https://doi.org/10.19030/ajbe.v3i3.399

Porter, S. R. (2011). Do college student surveys have any validity? *The Review of Higher Education*, *35*(1), 45–76. doi:10.1353/rhe.2011.0034.

Rivera, L. A., & Tilcsik, A. (2019). Scaling down inequality: Rating scales, gender bias, and the architecture of evaluation. *American Sociological Review, 84*(2), 248–274. https://doi.org/10.1177/0003122419833601

Tang, T. L., & Tang, T. L. (1987, Spring). A correlation study of students' evaluations of faculty performance and their self-ratings in an instructional setting. *College Student Journal, 21*, 90–97. https://files.eric.ed.gov/fulltext/ED279981.pdf

Trout, P. (2000). Flunking the test: The dismal record of student evaluations. *Academe, 86*(4), 58–61. Retrieved from https://search.proquest.com/openview/30241 9a688adf454d7f9c2e61c9cc521/1.pdf?pq-origsite=gscholar&cbl=41824

Valsan, C., & Sproule, R. (2008). The invisible hands behind the student evaluation of teaching: The rise of the new managerial elite in the governance of higher education. *Journal of Economic Issues, 42*(4), 939–958. https://doi.org/10.1080/00213624.2008.11507197

Waters, M., Kemp, E., & Pucci, A. (1988). High and low faculty evaluations: Descriptions by students. *Teaching of Psychology, 15*(4), 203–204. https://doi.org/10.1207/s15328023top1504_7

12 Validity and the Impacts of Subjectivity

Do Strong Opinions and Preconceived Notions Influence the Evaluation Process?

Both Paulus and Angela are department heads who were required to meet yearly at the college level to discuss faculty merit and to determine which instructors would receive a limited number of salary bonuses and awards. Each department head traditionally acted as a strong advocate for their own people. Angela advanced three female instructors. Paulus objected, claiming the three had lower student evaluations than his preferred instructors. Angela countered, "You can't make that claim. The evaluations are biased against women. Everyone knows that." Paulus replied, "Not so. If anything, the students overrate some of the women." The dean intervened, "Perhaps you both are reading your own interests into the evaluations."

Not everyone agrees on what SET validly measures, and the dean is correct; there has been a tendency to interpret the evaluations based on personal opinions and interests. However, does this modify the validity of decisions based on SET?

Strong Opinions

The SET literature, although complex, is often summarized by writers with strong opinions about the evaluation process.

A defender (Cranton, 2001) of the evaluations stated, "The *fact* (emphasis hers) that student ratings are generally reliable and valid is an outcome of at least three factors" (p. 15). Defenders of the present system insist their defense of SET is fact based, and the evaluation process is valid and useful. For an overview of evidence for their optimism, look at the generally excellent research of Herbert Marsh and the comprehensive reviews compiled by William Cashin (Hoyt & Cashin, 1977; Cashin, 1988, 1989, 1995, 1996; Cashin & Downey, 1992; Sixbury & Cashin, 1995). This body of work helped create a strong positive consensus. So much so that some, such as Theall and Franklin (2001), wondered why others stubbornly refused to embrace the procedure. After advancing several hypotheses, they warned critics that their negative attitudes could lead to pathological behavior and serious psychological problems. They did not acknowledge that a negative orientation toward the evaluation process may be based on empirical evidence, logic, and/or years of practical experience.

Others, however, were equally emphatic in their criticism of SET. One critic, after presenting a list of problems, concluded, "I expect that teacher ratings will reduce teachers' interest in helping people learn, while reducing student responsibility" (Armstrong, 1998, p. 1224). Stake (1997), a law professor at Indiana University, maintained that SET undermines the students' trust in the instructor, a point echoed by Gray and Berman (2003). At the same time, SET diverts attention away from "the message" of education onto a focus of action and special effects, and changes the instructor's behavior for the worse. Some, like Moore (2009), presented a long list of concerns identified in the literature that would invalidate SET. According to Stake, these consequences are serious enough that almost anything to undermine the SET administrative procedure ought to be done.

One of the consequences of this strong, and in some cases emotional, dichotomy is a propensity for users and researchers to make assumptions about the evaluations that are not warranted by the research or by logic.

Validity and Logic (The "Duh" Factor)

At times, emphatic positions have led to a necessity of researching what would be obvious if studying something less immediate to its practitioners. There has been a tendency for both faculty and administrators to take their preexisting assumptions about SET for granted without giving much thought about the resultant contradictions. When Valen Johnson's (2003) book was reviewed in the *Wall Street Journal*, the writer, upon reading that students give higher evaluations to teachers who give them higher grades, was reported to have issued an editorial "duh." The same response was made by an interested student, "His [Johnson's] exhaustive quantitative study, which I highly recommend to statistics majors and chronic insomniacs like myself, gives bales of empirical support to a number of 'duh' observations" (Gillum, 2004). Many, for example, appeared to be surprised when it was discovered that students would give purposeful misinformation on the evaluations (Clayson & Haley, 2011). The same institutions that require instructors to be present during an examination because of the fear of students cheating were and are accepting SET information at face value.

Much of the "duh" factor seems to be related to an almost subconscious assumption that the student evaluation of teaching must, on some level, be valid or (for a critic) invalid. These assumptions may be explained with a distinction between deductive and inductive knowledge made by Kors (1998). Deductive knowledge is what logically follows from a certain premise created or found in authoritative sources, which are then applied to the results of experience. Inductive knowledge is what logically follows from experience. Many researchers of SET appear to be interpreting their experience of SET in a deductive fashion, which can create interesting lapses in logic even the peer-review process of major publications does not eliminate. In one example, Feistauer and Richter (2018) found a high association between likability and SET. They concluded, "Likability seems to exert a substantial bias on student evaluation of teaching" (p. 168). Why assume likability is a bias rather than the essence of SET? Murray (1983) conducted a carefully crafted study on the relationship between instructor characteristics and SET, and found that instructors who received higher evaluations did teach differently in the classroom from instructors receiving lower ratings. He concluded "classroom behaviors" influenced the evaluations more than personality or popularity. He had found, however, that much of the ratings were associated with enthusiasm and rapport, factors which are highly related to personality, and which, as his own study implied, would influence popularity. Murray, in his introduction, assumed the SET process was valid, and with this mindset, saw visible classroom enthusiasm and rapport as an external teaching asset rather than a reflection of an internal characteristic of the individual instructor. In fairness to Murray, his research was conducted before newer studies found a large and substantial personality contribution in the evaluations.

The unquestioned assumption that the student evaluation of teaching must, on some level, be a valid or invalid measure of teaching can be seen in research conclusions, even in carefully crafted studies (see McGowan & Graham, 2009; Zhao & Gallant, 2012 as examples). John Centra, who made substantial contributions to the study of SET over a 30-year period, made the following observation, "Only those teachers who rated themselves much better than did their students appear to have changed after receiving mid-semester feedback" (Centra, 1972, p. 23). However, he did not determine if teachers had changed. He was instead measuring student responses on a SET. It is a common error to tautologically validate SET responses by utilizing SET responses.

> This writer once had a conversation with an administrator who stated a certain new faculty member was not teaching well. The evidence was a low average on a SET instrument. When asked what the SET was measuring, the administrator honestly replied, "I don't have a clue." This elicited the next logical question, "So we don't know how ____ is teaching?" "No," the administrator replied, "he isn't teaching well because his evaluations are low." Evaluations are so automatically and mechanically applied that this very bright professional remained unaware of the contradiction and tautological error that was being made.

Logical inconsistencies are common in SET, with little attempt to resolve them. It would seem logical, for example, that an association would exist between being a "good" or "effective" instructor and instructor's knowledge of the material being taught. Consequently, many teachers would argue that doing research makes them better instructors. An active researcher is more likely to be current with the discipline, to have more information to impart to students, and should be able to guide students better within the discipline's community. However, there is no evidence that faculty research itself benefits or harms the evaluations (Feldman, 1987; Hattie & Marsh, 1996; Jackson, 1994; Marsh & Hattie, 2002). If SET is an accurate measure of "effective" and/or "good" teaching, it would be logical to assume either researchers don't share what they have learned through research with their students, or an instructor being current and knowledgeable has no effect on the evaluations, which is an hypothesis with some research support (Doyle, 1975; Halloun & Hestenes, 1985). Consider a small study by Thornton, Adams, and Sepehri (2010), who found no evidence for grading, workload, or the pace of the class being related to the evaluations. However, they found challenging classes that required student effort resulted in lower evaluations. How could grading, workload, and pace not be related to a class being "challenging?"

The evaluations should be related to what students learn. If so, then factors found to be associated with the evaluations should also be associated with learning. Many of them are not. Attractiveness, gender, being fluent, the experience of the instructor, and rigor have all been found to be associated with SET, but to have no significant impact on student learning (performance).

Evaluations and the Law

Another generally ignored area has important consequences for the SET process and its legal implications. A standard of legal action states evaluation policies must be rational within the meaning of established law. Logical lapses and serious questions of validity challenge the utilization of SET in cases involving tenure and promotion. As stated by Wines and Lau (2006),

> Research on student teaching evaluations is vast. An examination of this research demonstrates wide disagreements but also substantial consensus of authority for the proposition that student evaluations should be used only with extreme care, if at all, in making personnel decisions.
> (p. 167)

Yet, counter to this "substantial consensus" of the research, the instruments are utilized almost universally as summative instruments. The widening gap between the research and the implementation of SET is not only illogical, it has serious consequences. As one investigator (Haskell, 1997) noted, "There are multiple latent legal issues engendered by SEF (*student evaluations of faculty*)" (p. 8 of 32).

According to American law, the employer has the burden of demonstrating an evaluation is job-related and validly so (Wines & Lau, 2006). In a lawsuit, the defendant bears the burden of proving its claimed reason for action is the true basis for the action taken. The plaintiff only needs to produce evidence that a reasonable jury, after viewing the defendant's evidence, could find only for the defendant. However, the plaintiff never bears the burden of persuasion regarding the affirmative defenses (Brunarski vs. Miami Univ., 2018). Yet, according to this writer's experience of providing evidence in several cases, instead of the institution demonstrating the validity of their instruments, many times the faculty member needed to show evidence that the instruments are invalid. In almost all other areas of HR interaction, it is the responsibility of the institution utilizing a measuring instrument to demonstrate it has validity. Even this evidence would not be sufficient if the instrument contained items which were not admissible in a dispute. Suppose, as an example, a company found that a test was 100% accurate in predicting a worker's future success by asking a potential employee if they were male, their grandmother smoked, and if the applicant liked ham sandwiches. The results of that instrument would not be admissible even if it offered almost perfect predictability. This analogy is not extreme. Keep in mind what it means to find that SET instruments have questionable discriminant and divergent validity.

Even if SET scales are shown to be valid, the written comments of the students can present a problem. A Canadian court has ruled tenure decisions cannot be based solely on SETs in which the student respondents were unaware of the ramifications of their statements, and unions have argued that anonymous documents should not be part of an instructor's file (Haskell, 1997). A professor at an American university was denied tenure and she sued, claiming the student comments on her class reflected a hostile work environment and the students discriminated against her because of her ethnic background (Schmidt, 2017). In a recent case, a Canadian court went a step further by establishing that SETs were not to be used to measure teaching effectiveness for promotion or tenure (Flaberty, 2018). Relevant issues have also been raised in the UK (Jones, Gaffney-Rhys, & Jones, 2012).

Does It Matter?

Even with these problems, the evaluations are now strongly entrenched within the educational establishment. However, much of the thinking of the defenders of the SET system relies on older findings. Finkelstein (1995), writing in *The NEA 1995 Almanac of Higher Education*, which summarized the literature base at the time, stated the evaluation instruments are "highly valid." Finkelstein cites several sources to say that if bias exists, the effects are relatively small, with well-recognized and controllable patterns. This view is still widely held, especially in some sectors of academe. It is important to note that these conclusions were derived from data taken from respondents (students) who are currently 50 to 80 years of age. In general, newer research does not support Finkelstein's optimism. In fact, a more current meta-analysis stated, "This review . . . has shown that the utility and validity ascribed to the SET should continue to be called into question" (Spooren, Brockx, & Mortelmans, 2013, p. 629).

Some commentators, such as Machina (1987), dismiss any argument of what is being measured and seemingly take a purely perceptual, consumer orientation. He states, "when students underrate a faculty member, that means there is a breakdown in the teaching process somewhere and it does not mean the evaluation is an inaccurate measure of the thing it is really geared to measure" (p. 22). This broadminded position may be appropriate for young students, but becomes problematic in higher education. It implies faculty and students should have the same views of pedagogic theory and application, even when, as pointed out earlier, a common theme in the literature is the lack of student input into the SET procedure (Kember & Leung, 2008).

Summary

1 Even with a large research base, SET has created both supporters and critics with strong opinions about validity.
2 Practitioners and researcher alike harbor preconceived and relatively strong opinions and assumptions about SET, which influence research conclusions and applications.
3 SET has real-world consequences and creates, in some cases, logical, legal, and ethical dilemmas that have been generally ignored by both researchers and administrators.
4 On balance, it appears the existing SET paradigm is not sufficient to resolve the errors and questions raised by its utilization.

References

Armstrong, J. S. (1998). Are student ratings of instruction useful? *American Psychologist, 53*, 1223–1224. https://doi.org/10.1037/0003-066X.53.11.1223

Brunarski v. Miami Univ. (2018, January 26). Civil Action No. 1:16-cv-311. Retrieved from https://casetext.com/case/brunarski-v-miami-univ-2

Cashin, W. E. (1988). *Student ratings of teaching: A summary of the research* (IDEA Paper No. 20). Publication of the Center for Faculty Evaluation & Development, Division of continuing Education, Kansas State University. Retrieved from https://eric.ed.gov/?id=ED302567

Cashin, W. E. (1989). *Defining and evaluating college teaching* (IDEA Paper No. 21). Publication of the Center for Faculty Evaluation & Development, Division of continuing Education, Kansas State University. Retrieved from https://eric.ed.gov/?id=ED339731

Cashin, W. E. (1995). *Student ratings of teaching: The research revisited* (IDEA Paper No. 32). Publication of the Center for Faculty Evaluation & Development, Division of continuing Education, Kansas State University. Retrieved from https://files.eric.ed.gov/fulltext/ED402338.pdf

Cashin, W. E. (1996). *Developing an effective faculty evaluation system* (IDEA Paper No. 33). Publication of the Center for Faculty Evaluation & Development, Division of continuing Education, Kansas State University. Retrieved from https://files.eric.ed.gov/fulltext/ED395536.pdf

Cashin, W. E., & Downey, R. G. (1992). Using global student rating items for summative evaluation. *Journal of Educational Psychology, 84*(4), 563–572. https://doi.org/10.1037/0022-0663.84.4.563

Centra, J. A. (1972). *Two studies on the utility of student ratings for instructional improvement* (SIR Report No. 9). Princeton, NJ: Educational Testing Service.

Clayson, D. E., & Haley, D. A. (2011). Are students telling us the truth? A critical look at the student evaluation of teaching. *Marketing Education Review, 21*(2), 103–114. https://doi.org/10.2753/MER1052-8008210201

Cranton, P. (2001, Winter). Interpretive and critical evaluation. In C. Knapper & P. Cranton (Eds.), *New direction for teaching and learning: Fresh approaches to the evaluation of teaching* (Vol. 88, pp. 11–18). Retrieved from www.semanticscholar.org/paper/2-Interpretive-and-Critical-Evaluation-Cranton/ece84376628845862615833 1ae6268d68c9e21e7

Doyle, K. O. (1975). *Student evaluation of instruction.* Lexington, MA: Lexington Books.

Feistauer, D., & Richter, T. (2018). Validity of students' evaluations of teaching: Biasing effects of likability and prior subject interest. *Educational Evaluation, 59*, 168–178. https://doi.org/10.1016/j.stueduc.2018.07.009

Feldman, K. A. (1987). Research productivity and scholarly accomplishment of college teachers as related to their instructional effectiveness: A review and exploration. *Research in Higher Education, 26*, 227–298. https://doi.org/10.1007/BF00992241

Finkelstein, M. J. (1995). College faculty as teachers. In *The NEA 1995 almanac of higher education* (pp. 33–47). Washington, DC: National Education Association. Retrieved from https://eric.ed.gov/?id=ED378865

Flaberty, C. (2018, August 31). Arbitrating the use of student evaluations of teaching. *Inside Higher Ed, Quick Take.* Retrieved from www.insidehighered.com/quicktakes/2018/08/31/arbitrating-use-student-evaluations-teaching

Gillum, M. (2004, March 22). Grade inflation in humanities a dangerous trend. *The Chronicle (Duke University), Opinion.* Retrieved from http://dukechronicle.com/article/ grade-inflation-humanities-dangerous-trend

Gray, M., & Bermann, B. R. (2003, September–October). Student teaching evaluations: Inaccurate, demeaning, misused. *Academe*, 44–46. Retrieved from http://web.utk.edu/~senate/TeachingEvaluations.pdf

Halloun, I. A., & Hestenes, D. (1985). The initial knowledge state of college physics students. *American Journal of Physics, 53*(11), 1053–1055. https://doi.org/10.1119/1.14030

Haskell, R. E. (1997). Academic freedom, tenure, and student evaluation of faculty: Galloping polls in the 21st century. *Education Policy Analysis Archives, 5*(6). Retrieved from http://epaa.asu.edu/epaa/v5n6.html

Hattie, J., & Marsh, H. W. (1996). The relationship between research and teaching: A meta-analysis. *Review of Educational Research, 66*(4), 507–542. https://doi.org/10.3102/00346543066004507

Hoyt, D. P., & Cashin, W. E. (1977). *Development of the IDEA system* (IDEA Technical Report No. 1). Publication of the Center for Faculty Evaluation & Development, Division of continuing Education, Kansas State University. Retrieved from https://eric.ed.gov/?id=ED175303

Jackson, C. (1994). How personality profiling can change your life. *Physics World, 7*(4), 101–103. Retrieved from https://iopscience.iop.org/article/10.1088/2058-7058/7/4/49/pdf

Johnson, V. E. (2003). *Grade inflation: A crisis in college education.* New York: Springer.

Jones, J., Gaffney-Rhys, R., & Jones, E. (2012). Handle with care! An exploration of the potential risks associated with the publication and summative usage of student evaluation of teaching (SET) results. *Journal of Further and Higher Education*, *38*(1), 37–56. https://doi.org/10.1080/0309877X.2012.699514

Kember, D., & Leung, D. Y. P. (2008). Establishing the validity and reliability of course evaluation questionnaires. *Assessment & Evaluation in Higher Education*, *33*(4), 341–353. https://doi.org/10.1080/02602930701563070

Kors, A. C. (1998). The birth of the modern mind: The intellectual history of the 17th and 18th centuries. *The Great Courses*, Course #447, Lecture 13.

Machina, K. (1987, May–June). Evaluating student evaluations. *Academe*, 19–22. Retrieved from www.jstor.org/stable/40249936?seq=1

Marsh, H. W., & Hattie, J. (2002). The relation between research productivity and teaching effectiveness. *The Journal of higher Education*, *73*(5), 603–641. https://doi.org/10.1080/00221546.2002.11777170

McGowan, W. R., & Graham, C. R. (2009). Factors contributing to improved teaching performance. *Innovative Higher Education*, *34*, 161–171. https://doi.org/10.1007/s10755-009-9103-6

Moore, P. (2009). Why we should measure student learning: A glossary of collegiate corruption. In R. E. Flinn & D. L. Crumbly (Eds.), *Measure learning rather than satisfaction in higher education* (pp. 91–110). Sarasota, FL: American Accounting Association.

Murray, H. G. (1983). Low-inference classroom teaching behaviors and student ratings of college teaching effectiveness. *Journal of Educational Psychology*, *75*(1), 138–149. https://doi.org/10.1037/0022-0663.75.1.138

Schmidt, P. (2017). When students' bias taint reviewers of instruction. *The Chronicles of Higher Education, Insight Faculty*, A6–A7. Retrieved from www.chronicle.com/article/When-Students-Prejudices/238892

Sixbury, G. R., & Cashin, W. E. (1995). *Descriptions of database for the IDEA diagnostic form* (IDEA Technical Report No. 9). Publication of the Center for Faculty Evaluation & Development, Division of Continuing Education, Kansas State University.

Spooren, P., Brockx, B., & Mortelmans, D. (2013). On the validity of student evaluation of teaching: The state of the art. *Review of Educational Research*, *83*(4), 598–642. https://doi.org/10.3102/0034654313496870

Stake, J. E. (1997). Response to Haskell: Academic freedom. Tenure, and student evaluation of faculty. *Education Policy Archives*, *5*(8). Retrieved from www//epaa.asu.edu/epaa/v5n8.html

Theall, M., & Franklin, J. (2001). Looking for bias in all the wrong places: A search for truth or a witch hunt in student ratings of instruction? *New Directions for Institutional Research*, *27*(5), 45–56. https://doi.org/10.1002/ir.3

Thornton, B., Adams, M., & Sepehri, M. (2010). The impact of students' expectations of grades and perceptions of course difficulty, workload, and pace on faculty evaluations. *Contemporary Issues in Education Research*, *3*(12), 1–5. https://files.eric.ed.gov/fulltext/EJ1072684.pdf

Wines, W. A., & Lau, T. J. (2006). Article: Observations on the folly of using student evaluations of college teaching for faculty evaluation, pay, and retention decisions and its implication for academic freedom. *William and Mary Journal of Women and the Law, 13*(1), Article 4. Retrieved from http://scholarship.law. wm.edu/wmjowl/vol13/iss1/4.

Zhao, J., & Gallant, D. J. (2012). Student evaluation of instruction in higher education: Exploring issues of validity and reliability. *Assessment & Evaluation in Higher Education, 37*(2), 227–235. https://doi.org/10.1080/02602938.2010. 523819

13 Introducing a Likability Hypothesis

What Do the Evaluations Actually Measure?

Ian walked into his colleague's office and sat down hard. "What's the matter?" Beth asked. "You look upset." Ian replied, "I just got my student evaluations back, and for the third year in a row, I have one of the lowest evals in our department. I am frustrated and confused." Ian explained he had taught at a large private university with high academic standards before coming to his current school. He was ranked in the top 5% of all faculty by the students. He had also taught some classes at an elite local college and received outstanding reviews. "Not only that," he continued, "when I lecture or speak in the community or before professional groups, I am always told what a good teacher I am." He laughed, "Some have even told me how lucky my students are to have me for their teacher, and look at these . . . according to them, I'm one of the worst teachers in our entire department. One of the reasons I became a professor was my belief I could teach well." Beth smiled, "Maybe this group of students just doesn't like you." "Well, maybe so," Ian replied, "but still . . . am I a good teacher or a bad one?"

This is an excellent question. How could one group of students consistently view a person as a good teacher, while another group consistently sees the same person as a bad teacher? Is one of the groups wrong? If so, which? One could argue that being a good teacher depends upon who is being taught, but surely there is some commonality that would allow a differentiation between teaching ability that is not dependent upon the immediate student sitting in front of an instructor. In fact, almost all the research on SET makes this very assumption. Is it possible the problem is the assumption itself?

Introduction

We can now return to the original question:

What Does SET Actually Measure?

A number of different hypotheses have been advanced, but there is only one that is consistent with all the evidence. As demonstrated by the literature, almost every aspect of the evaluations has produced contradictory research findings. Instead of assuming certain findings are correct and others are wrong, it would be more advantageous to advance a hypothesis suggesting SET measures what it has actually been found to measure. The research has demonstrated, for example, that some students reward learning and some do not; and some students have shown a gender bias, and some have not. All of these responses can be logically connected by assuming the evaluations measure student perceptions, and the scale created by SET can be summarized by the word "likability." Overall, and on average, the evaluations measure whether an instructor and/or class is "liked" by some particular group of students, at some point in time. Perhaps a better term was one used in the past when it was said a professor was "popular" with his or her students. Ironically, the word "popular" is more consistent with recent research findings than the terms "good," "best," or "effective," which are now widely utilized. This paradigm change has some interesting and important consequences. Numerous research efforts have attempted to identify factors which are related to the evaluations and then compare these to some concept, theory, or application of instruction. Finding this difficult, some researchers have compared their findings with the instruments themselves, suggesting that if the process is taken back far enough, some instrument somewhere validly measured "good" or "effective" teaching. Adjustment and "norming" have been called for to correct factors or variables that should not logically be related to "effective" teaching. All of this suggests SET is a valid measure of teaching at its core but is "tainted" by other factors. That arguably is not true. The instruments appear, at their basic levels, to be a measure of popularity in much the same sense as how the term was used before the advent of SET.

Almost 50 years ago, and given the research which existed at the time, a likability hypothesis was firmly rejected by most compilers (see Page, 1974), but their conclusion was based as much on supposition as research findings. Page states,

> To the degree that it is possible to pin down this idea [likability] it is probably untrue, but it is difficult to operationalize it. Students are well

able to differentiate between personality and teaching behavior, and so they are unlikely to be misled by superficial characteristics.

(p. 67)

It is an arguable contention student are "able" to differentiate between personality and teaching behavior, but the research reviewed here indicates that irrespective of being "able," students seldom do differentiate. Further, a likability hypothesis does not rule out the possibility of finding excellent instructors who are also likable and even popular. In fact, the entire SET process is dependent upon it.

The real research question, and the one which would best explain the mountain of data collected over the last 70 years, is simply this:

What is Related to any Given Student, or Group of Students, Liking an Instructor?

Too many administrators and researchers have been seduced by the language. If they are dealing with the "student evaluation of teaching," then their findings must have something to do with "teaching." The lack of convergent and discriminant validity is then seen as the result of errors that are contaminating the core validity of the instruments rather than logical and expected components of student perception.

Problems Resolved by the Hypothesis

As long as SET is seen as a measure of "good" or "effective" teaching, it remains full of contradictions and paradoxes. At the turn of the century, Aleamoni (1999) published a list of 16 "common myths" about the evaluation process. Each of these "myths" referred to research findings and commentaries that would suggest SET was not a valid measure of good or effective teaching. These, he states, were not real, but were attempts to "impugn" the value of the ratings. Each of these 16 points can be resolved logically by looking at the evaluation process as a measure of likability instead of attempting to ignore findings which counter the assumption SET is a valid measure of good instruction.

So far, chapters of this book have summarized different areas of research, and each presented contradictions created by the assumption that SET is a measure of actual teaching.

1   There is no acceptable argument which would imply men and women, on average, are not equally good teachers, but there remains substantial evidence they receive different evaluations.

2 The students' perception of an instructor's personality is highly related to SET, yet the instructor's perception of his or her own personality is not. Further, there appears to be little relationship between how students see themselves and the evaluations.
3 The Dr. Fox Effect appears to be alive and well. Students are influenced by instructor characteristics that have little to do with good instruction, but are instead related to social and personal variables consistent with likability-based social interactions. What valid argument could be made that would suggest physically attractive instructors are better teachers, or members of one race are better instructors than another?
4 It appears a certain percentage of students will be purposely untruthful when responding to the evaluations. An objective observer of an external reality is unlikely to do this.
5 A student seeking knowledge and expertise would be expected to select and reward teachers who have a proven track record. Yet the evaluations appear to be unrelated to the teaching experience of the instructor and to the instructor's knowledge of the subject matter as reflected by involvement in the discipline. Being a professor appears to be the only profession in which years of practice do not improve performance.
6 It would be expected that students would learn more and be better prepared for subsequent classes and their careers if their instructors were challenging and rigorous, both with grades and course content. Yet the evaluations are generally unrelated, or negatively related, to rigor.
7 Almost universally, instructors who give higher grades get higher evaluations. Students appear to reward instructors who reward them, even if the quality of instruction remains constant. There are exceptions, which appear to be related to interpersonal characteristics of both the students and instructor.
8 The purpose of schooling is assumed to be related to what students learn. Good teachers should be expected to expedite this expectation. A measure of good teaching should therefore be related to learning. Presently, it is not.
9 If asked why teachers should be evaluated, the response would universally assume evaluation would lead to improved teaching. There is little evidence an institutional SET process leads to better instruction, as measured by SET.
10 Before an instrument can be seen as valid, it must first be shown to be reliable. SET is both reliable and unreliable, depending upon how it is utilized. If an instrument is a good measure of an objective reality, how can it have both inter-item reliability and between-rater unreliability at the same time?

11 In like fashion, how can a valid instrument have convergent validity and be lacking in discriminant and divergent validity?

All of these issues can be resolved by assuming they are a result of error and prejudice, but it is not necessary to do so. They can be resolved without the need for the negative appraisal of others' research and motives. The likability hypothesis states students are responding with their perception of what they like, at that moment of time, filtered through an assessment instrument. SET is very much like a customer satisfaction survey administered by service providers.

Likability and Learning

The troubling conclusions and illogical assumptions created by the difficulty of finding a relationship between the evaluations and gains in learning can serve as an example of how the likability hypothesis can clarify other problems. Consistent with existing mindsets, a logical person would conclude the evaluations are a measure of an instructor's ability to improve student learning, but both direct and interactive factors related to learning have been shown to be largely independent of SET. Even the most ardent defenders of the evaluations state that whatever SET is measuring accounts for only 4–6% of the variance of associated learning. In statistical terms, even these strong advocates of the validity of the evaluations admit 95% of the differences in the evaluations are unrelated to learning. The majority of modern research finds no relationship at all. Ironically, the SET process does not attempt to measure learning in that the evaluations do not require the testing of students. At best, SET gives an imperfect, second-order representation of the *perception* of learning.

In fact, on a very foundational level, SET actually has little to do with learning. Unless there is an association between something students like with some subjective perception of learning, we would expect no relationship at all.

> **SET is not designed to be a measure of an objective reality. It is a measure of student perceptions.**

If a student likes what happens in a classroom, or with an instructor, or even some social or cultural variable that might be perceptually related to what the student is reporting within the constraints of a particular questionnaire, and some of it is related to another measure of subjective or objective learning, then there will be an association between the evaluations and learning. Finding this relationship, or not finding it, is not a contaminate of the true essence of the evaluations. The actual core is a summation of any particular group's average perception of what they like or dislike.

The population responding to SET instruments are "students." They should be expected to have interests a "student" would have. Being a student should be related, at least statistically, with a preference for learning, and the perception of learning is associated with the evaluations. The inability of the instruments to generally identify instructors whose students are learning from those whose students do not learn, indicates, irrespective of instructor effectiveness, that students are reacting to how well they "like" what the instructor represented, consistent with the students' nomological expectations. Further, it is reasonable to expect that not all students would like the discipline and effort needed to master learning. In fact, on average, instructors who teach material that is difficult, such as math and physics, receive lower evaluations, seemingly irrespective of how the average instructor teaches. Students also have other competing interests. A student, for example, may want a degree, but not necessarily want the education associated with the degree (Clifford, 1994). In addition, for the instruments to be valid measures of what students learned in a class, the students would have to be able to objectively scale learning. There is little evidence this occurs.

The discussion of learning also allows us to address a question that has bothered educators for some time: *How would a student evaluate an instructor from whom they learned a great deal, but who they thoroughly disliked?* This question cannot be adequately answered by saying some students would rate the instructor highly. The actual usage of SET utilizes summative or mean scores. Nor can we simply assume being disliked makes an instructor unsuccessful. All we will learn from SET is what the majority of students like or dislike.

Clarifications for Research

The likability hypothesis leads to new insights in both the design and the interpretation of research. As discussed previously, there is a "duh effect" in the SET literature, characterized by detailed investigations into factors outsiders simply take for granted, such as a grade-evaluation relationship. Tautological errors are also common, in which conclusions consistent with objective theories are suggested directly in the face of contradictory evidence.

Consider the question of gender. Defenders of traditional SET validity assume the instruments are an objective measure of the instructor and/or the instructor's class. Therefore, any change in the evaluation, when there was no change in instruction or the instructor, has to be seen as a contaminating factor that needs to be eliminated or controlled. As opposed to this, gender bias under the assumption of likability assumes students' perceptions will reflect the bias of their culture. This would lead to a new stream of research, properly looking at cultural differences and their implications for instruction.

The likability hypothesis changes the evaluation schemata and the corresponding mindset driving the focus of SET research.

Counter Arguments

A number of arguments could be made challenging the hypothesis that SET is, in essence, a perceptual measure of likability.

Likable Traits Lead to Better Teaching

The likability hypothesis could be countered by positing the traits students list for an "effective" instructor, such as being knowledgeable, dedicated, caring, dynamic, etc., are related to "good" teaching because they lead to ... what? Better prepared students? Instructors who are better teachers? More learning? But SET has not been shown to increase the quality of instruction, the students' level of preparedness, or even what students may have learned. Assuming likable traits constitute the substance of "good" teaching leads to an argument that becomes almost immediately tautological. The finding that instructors with average evaluations have a higher association between learning and SET than instructors with higher or lower evaluations (Galbraith, Merrill, & Kline, 2012) indicates that the personal and instructional aspects of an instructor may be related to learning, but only as second-order, tangential variables.

Good Teaching and Being Liked Are Synonymous

Another related counter argument to the hypothesis would read: Why wouldn't a teacher who is liked actually be a better teacher? Consider an instructor who is very well liked by graduate students, but not well liked by undergraduate students. Would not that instructor be a good teacher for graduate students and not a good teacher for undergraduates? If a sophomore student reports, "I dislike the way he teaches. I can't understand what he is trying to do in class," no matter how successful that instructor is with graduate students, is he still not a good teacher for sophomores? Therefore, the SET is actually measuring the effectiveness of instruction. The argument appears sound, but it has the same flaw that has driven much of the SET research. What is meant by "effective?" If this hypothetical instructor were to make presentations in the sophomore class the students liked, would that imply they are now learning more, or are better prepared for future endeavors, or . . . they now simply don't dislike the instructor? Given the fundamental finding that SET has little relationship to these important variables, all we have *from the students' evaluation* is they don't "like" his presentation. If SET were utilized to correct the instructor's in-class approach, which most administrators would recommend, that correction could facilitate an increase in what students learn. However, the finding that SET results do not measure improved instruction, combined with the lack of association with objective learning, returns the argument to its genesis. The instruments are not validly measuring any hypothetical improvement in student performance. We would have to test the students to determine that, which again returns us to the original hypothesis that SET fundamentally measures student perceptions, translated into a metric of likability.

Students Are Best Qualified to Evaluate

What about the argument students are best qualified to evaluate teaching because they are the ones present in the classroom? Page (1974) utilized this argument by quoting Aristotle, "You get a better notion of the merits of the dinner from the dinner guests than you do from the cook" (p. 28). Instead of weakening the likability hypothesis, Aristotle's quote actually reinforces it. First, what does the term "merit" mean, and to what does it refer? Second, the guests are actually relating their perception of the dinner, not of the cook. Their evaluation of the dinner is based on their perceptions, not necessarily on the quality of the dinner or about the chef who produced it. Again, we are back to the idea of likability. Some may have liked or disliked the dinner based on any number of variables, including cost, atmospherics, or even on the social interaction among the diners. It could still be argued that the chef produced the situation(s) that created the perceptions, but we never get to measure these because we are very busy attempting to measure the perceptions of the guests. Using this analogy, we are not evaluating teaching – we might not even be evaluating *anything* the teacher has actually done. We are attempting to measure the perceptions of the students to discover what they like.

The experience in the classroom argument must also deal with other concerns. Philip Stark, professor of statistics at UC Berkeley, after pointing out statistical problems with the evaluations, wrote, "Student comments provide valuable data about the students' experiences. Whether they are a good measure of teaching effectiveness is another matter" (Stark, 2013).

Even with his supporting declaration separating student experience from measures of teacher effectiveness, we are still left with the question: How do we know what the "student experience" was? The evaluations reflect, using a format typically not selected by the students, the students' *perceptions* of their experience. These perceptions may or may not be accurate. Perceptual distortion is an area which has been extensively researched. A Google Scholar search of "perceptual defense: problems with eyewitness" generated almost 7,000 hits. A search of "perceptual defense" created over 200,000. Again, even if SET is not a measure of effective teaching, it remains a measure of student perceptions, complete with all the cultural, social, psychological, and neural intricacies that surround perception.

A summative administrative problem also arises with this counterargument. Consider a case in which students report an instructor violates protocols such as arriving to class late, being lax in returning materials, and, in general, misbehaving, but the students love the instructor. Or the counter example of an instructor who has impeccable pedagogic behavior, but whom the students dislike. In the first case, an administrator is likely to say, "The students like you, but you are not being a good teacher." In the second, the instructor is likely to hear, "You're doing a good job in the classroom even if the students don't like you." Note that even if the students are capable of objective perceptions of an external reality, the students' input, if incompatible with the views of a summative agent, are likely to be discounted as mere perceptions.

> The likability hypothesis does not eliminate the possibility that a well-liked instructor might be a very good teacher based on any number of legitimate pedagogic standards, but that SET is not measuring these; it is giving a measure of student perceptions cognitively organized into a schema reflecting how well the instructor is liked.

Students Are Customers

A person could still argue, even if the likability hypothesis is true, that the evaluations are a valid measure of good teaching for utilitarian reasons. In a customer-service relationship, the "service" must be "liked" by the customer. It is simply basic marketing. Happy students are likely to re-enroll and are less likely to resist tuition increases. In terms of academic management, having instructors who keep students happy is a plus. Anything which drives students away is to be avoided. This argument sidesteps the issue.

It essentially says we do not care what aspect of instruction SET measures as long as the students are happy. There are practical, societal, and philosophical problems with the student-as-customer orientation (Clayson & Haley, 2005). While it may have immediate benefits, the long-term consequences are arguably not beneficial for the students, the school, or society.

Common Usage of SET Assumes a Likability Hypothesis

In conventional usage and language, it is common for administrators and faculty, and even some researchers, to refer to SET findings as student perceptions without logically connecting their language to their conclusions. This can be seen in how the instruments are pragmatically utilized by administrators. An interesting example was demonstrated by a dean who was required to evaluate his faculty. He claimed to have read every student comment on the evaluation instrument and then looked at the following evidence: 1) The scores on the SET instrument, 2) specific student comments about learning and skill development, and 3) the grade point average for the class. The likability hypothesis states that the SET score will largely be a result of likability, but can a likeable instructor still produce academic achievement and, at the same time, keep grades below or near norms? The answer is obviously yes. However, this story contains several caveats. First, the dean is admitting the SET scores themselves are a measure of likability. He is essentially saying that the instructor is still liked by his or her students even though other academic goals are met. This admission calls into question the evaluation's ability to measure, or be compatible with, desired academic goals. Second, the dean is assuming student comments about learning and academic achievement are providing important information of some sort, because he insists on reading them all. Lastly, the dean's challenge creates a certain amount of irony. Why use the time-consuming and expensive SET procedure if he is going to use his own judgment, much as if the evaluation did not exist in its present form? At this point, we can give an answer to this question. The administrator did not have an interest in the evaluations because they indicated who was a good teacher. He determined that himself. He was interested in the evaluations because they told him who the students like.

The acknowledgement of the likability hypothesis is found in many common summative decisions. This writer was recently made aware of a communique between two sister universities in different countries. A visiting professor was recommended for another teaching opportunity simply because, "The students liked him."

The Bottom Line

The SET process measures the perceptions of students filtered through an instrument typically not of the student's design. The evaluations are not an objective measure of either the instructor or the class. The evaluation process is not contaminated by intervening variables that need to be corrected. The evaluations are measuring what they are, by default, designed to measure, i.e., whether students "like" or "dislike" any particular instructional aspect elicited by the evaluation process.

In summation, the contradictions found in much of the SET research are better explained by assuming a likability hypothesis than by suggesting the instruments measure an instructor's ability to be an "effective" teacher.

Summary

1 SET is composed of an assessment of student perceptions.
2 The scale produced by these perceptions can best be described as a "likability" scale.
3 The SET process is not contaminated by intervening variables. It is a measure of the average perceptions of how well an instructor or class is liked by any given group of students. These perceptions may or may not be related to any institutional or theoretical concept of effective teaching.

References

Aleamoni, L. M. (1999). Student rating myths versus research facts from 1924 to 1998. *Journal of Personnel Evaluation in Education*, *13*(2), 153–166. https://doi.org/10.1023/A:1008168421283

Clayson, D. E., & Haley, D. A. (2005). Marketing models in education: Students as customers, products, or partners. *Marketing Education Review*, *15*(1), 1–10. https://doi.org/10.1080/10528008.2005.11488884

Clifford, D. (1994). The "customer-driven" classroom: A rebuttal. *The Teaching Professor*, *8*(9), 1–2.

Galbraith, C. S., Merrill, G. B., & Kline, D. M. (2012). Are student evaluations of teaching effectiveness valid for measuring student learning outcomes in business related classes? A neural network and Bayesian analyses. *Research in Higher Education*, *53*(3), 353–374. https://doi.org/10.1007/s11162-011-9229-0

Page, C. F. (1974). *Student evaluation of teaching: The American experience*. London: Society for Research into Higher Education.

Stark, P. (2013, October 14). Do student evaluations measure teaching effectiveness? *Berkeley Blog (Economics)*. Retrieved from https://blogs.berkeley.edu/2013/10/14/do-student-evaluations-measure-teaching-effectiveness/#comments

14 Justifications of the Likability Hypothesis

What Are the Justifications and Implications of the Likability Hypothesis?

Aisha Samaha is a visiting professor from Lebanon. She had an interview with her dean after her first semester. During their conversation, the dean remarked how pleased he was with her first semester teaching evaluations. "They are well within the top 10% of all our faculty," he remarked. "I am also pleased, but surprised," Aisha replied. "I didn't think they would be that positive. I really haven't done a very good job. Sometimes I get my English mixed up and I am embarrassed, and that just makes things worse." "Well," the dean said, looking at her evaluation summary, "the students seem to like you. They remarked how gracious you are, and how you made Lebanon more real for them." Aisha smiled and replied, "I am pleased it went well, but next semester I will be a better teacher."

In what way will Aisha be a better teacher? By improving her language skills? By giving more detailed and correct information of her home country? Perhaps, but the dean is correct; her students liked her because they found her humble and "gracious." Further, the students live in a culture in which it would be inappropriate to appear prejudicial toward a female visiting professor with a Muslim background.

As a person looks through the SET literature, a pattern begins to emerge. It is possible on many occasions to predict a research outcome, or to explain inconsistencies, by looking at SET, not as a measure of teaching, but as a measure of what students like and dislike. The research supports, and this book argues, that the closest universal term captured by the SET process and expressed in its scales is "likability."

Psychological and Perceptual Justification (SET as a Measure of Students)

The likability hypothesis assumes SET is a compilation of student perceptions, a contention already held by some modern compilers (Hativa, 2014). However, it is not necessarily true that these perceptions are "caused" by the instructor or anything the instructor has done or may be doing. Several lines of reasoning suggest student perceptions of instruction can *only* be seen as a measurement of students.

Statistical Consensus and Perception

Berk (2013) outlines the appropriate response rates for the SET process to be statistically acceptable for summative and formative purposes. Let us examine this necessity in light of the likability hypothesis. A group of people see an unusual moving light in the sky. One person says it is an alien UFO, another says it is a secret military aircraft on maneuvers, and a third says it is weather phenomena. To estimate what percent of the population would say it is a UFO requires a measurement of a reasonable number of people to reduce the sampling error to an acceptable level. Nevertheless, a sample size of a million or a sample size of one are equally valid in determining if the light in the sky *really* was an alien UFO. In other words, it can be determined that a certain percent of people believe the phenomena is a UFO, but we cannot determine from this data if what they experienced was a UFO. Similarly, an acceptable rate of responses on a SET are only applicable if we assume we are measuring something about students and not instructors.

Suppose 80 out of 100 students in a class gave a low evaluation because they felt their instructor was aloof and uncaring. The instructor says he is neither. He cares very much about his students, but he comes from a culture in which ranking professionals do not display public emotions, and he admits to being somewhat shy and innately has a hard time interacting in large groups. Is the students' reaction correct? As long as only student perceptions are being rated, and the students are not being purposefully duplicitous, yes. Is their rating of the instructor correct? No. The students believe he is aloof and uncaring based on their reactions to their own culturally based perceptions, not to what the instructor *is*.

The Limits of Objectivity (Ideology)

Administratively, the likability hypothesis is ironically reaffirmed. The perception of students is important to universities and academic programs.

However, what is the reaction when student perceptions do not match institutional goals or standards? What if students, for example, disliked black female instructors or other instructors who may come under the rubric of diversity? In these cases, it would be assumed students' reactions, although valuable, are incorrect and need to be adjusted. In other words, the students' evaluations are now seen as perceptions and not as reflecting the valid reality of their instructors, or of the value of their instruction.

Even without questioning the existence of a reality separate from the mind (stimuli do have a source), it remains problematic to suggest the instructor "portrayed," "induced," or otherwise *caused* the label or value placed on the perception in the students' minds. The perceptions and the interpretations of the students belong to them. If the students had come from the same culture as the instructor, their responses might differ substantially. Differences in how the students were raised, their gender, their expectations of a classroom environment, and hundreds of other nature-nurture variables could have influenced their perception of the instructor. Even if they all experienced the same stimuli, they did not all experience the same perception. Perception is ultimately created by the observer, not by the stimuli.

Physical and Philosophical Justification (Rejection of Student-As-Thermometer Model)

The likability hypothesis argues SET is a measure of students and may not be a measure of instructors or even instruction. Along with the sensation and perception implications, there is a philosophical argument which would suggest SET cannot measure actual instruction because of epistemological imperfections, and even because of ontological fundamentals.

The Nature of Perception

For thousands of years, philosophers have considered the problem of perception. Plato thought the human mind was capable of accessing reality, but only imperfectly. Hence, his allegory of a cave, i.e., we only know reality as shadows cast on a cave's wall. Plato, however, was unaware of the knowledge we now have of the sense-perceptual system, which both simplifies and complicates Plato's concept. The mind is truly within the cave of the skull and only "sees" the input of the senses. What we experience of the world is a product of some function of the "real" world modified by our senses and reconstructed by the mind. We see a wall as a solid barrier, even though physics and mathematics tell us it is made largely of empty space. If we could see in radio waves, it would be transparent. Since we do not, we experience it as a solid opaque object. We also perceive things that do not exist outside of our minds. There is no color or sound outside of perception. We also dream and have hallucinations. None of this implies reality does not exist, but we perceive reality only within a context bounded by a perceptual system. We attach names and even emotions to color, and beautiful music can create strong emotions, but these exist only in our minds. Truth is created by a construction of sense-perceptions and associations of memory and experience. These are influenced by an almost infinite combination of biology, past perceptions, interpersonal and cultural factors, and by an aversion to contradictions. The truth of any object for any given observer is always dependent on these judgments (Cahoone, 2010).

With apologies to any philosopher who may be reading, we could see the reality of anything referred to as "good" or "effective" teaching in light of this discussion. There is no way a student can objectively know if an instructor is an "effective" teacher except through the sense-perceptual system of the individual, modified by his or her historical and cultural experiences. All of which means: a) we cannot single out the instructor as a source of objective measurement, and b) "good" or "effective" teaching is mind and culturally dependent, and is created by how it is perceived. "Good" and/or "effective" instruction must be seen as a perception created by the student.

A Temperature Analogy

The general use of SET assumes some sort of validating procedure and/or device to assess student perceptions. The problem thus created is analogous to attempting to measure temperature. To do so, the first task is to agree on a definition. What is temperature? However, that question does not stand alone. It is uniquely linked to two others. Can the object of the definition be measured? And, what is the purpose of the measurement?

We may select a method of measuring temperature because our definition links it physically to other events. Temperature is the average kinetic energy of the molecules in a substance. The kinetic energy of molecules and the pressure of a gas at a constant volume are directly related. If the pressure of the captured gas is reduced to zero, the temperature would also be zero. Therefore, a temperature scale can be created with zero representing the absence of temperature. This is the Kelvin ratio scale derived directly from mathematically measurable, physical phenomena. Temperature, thus defined, can be measured independent of any subjective human perception.

Suppose, instead, temperature was defined as a human sense-perception. Some things *feel* warmer or cooler. Attempts to measure perceptual temperature would at best create an ordinal scale. Further, two or more people experiencing the same environment would not necessarily *feel* the same temperature. Even if they did, they may report it differently because of personal and/or cultural differences. We would, however, expect a correspondence between raters, which, paradoxically, could occur because of the actual temperature, *or* because of similar personal and cultural factors. The evaluations should be correlated even if there is no exact scale. To a certain extent, we are now measuring the raters.

Now, we ask people to rate how comfortable or pleasing a temperature is. At best, we are now measuring a reaction to temperature, which could be modified by genetics, acclimatization, upbringing, and dozens of other factors. Now we are evaluating raters. The actual temperature, as an indicator of kinetic energy, has become a second or even a third-order variable.

In this analogy, students cannot be seen as thermometers of an external reality. There is no doubt SET creates a measure of the students themselves. SET does not measure instructors or an objective standard of instruction. It attempts to scale the student's perception, which may be related to instructors or instruction. Commonalities between students are as likely to be a creation of their common nature-nurture experience as it is of any objective measure of "good" or "effective" instruction. As stated by researcher Beau Lotto,[1] "no one is an outside observer of nature."

This being so, why are we so surprised when we find student sense-perceptions in SET? Perhaps we cling to the student-as-thermometer model because we find the alternative disquieting.

Research Implications

The change in mindset introduced by the likability hypothesis opens up a universe of research options with both practical and philosophical implications. Given any group of students at any given time, what should students "like" about a class or the instructor of the class?

Personal Factors Will Be Evident in SET

Finding cognitive dissonance, attribution, manifestations of ego, and other effects related to self-concepts in the evaluations should be expected and not seen as bias or errors.

Factors Which Influence How Well a Person is Liked Will Be Found in the Evaluations

People, in general, like others who they judge to be caring, sympathetic, and helpful. Most people like to be exposed to a positive and enjoyable interaction with someone skilled in offering an entertaining event; the exact situation found in the famous "Dr. Fox" example. Halo effects should be found in the evaluations.

Social Class Differences Will Influence the Evaluations

Students arrive with social class values which influence their attitudes, expectations, choice of schools, and the fundamental reason for gaining a higher education (DeAngelis, 2015). Are the students there to get a job, widen their horizons, or build useful connections for the future? One observer[2] wrote of working-class students, "I found that many of the students were quite surprised to learn that they might be expected to 'enjoy reading' or that students who are ready for college 'read for pleasure.'" These students would "like" different characteristics in instructors than would those from a different social class.

Cultural Variables Will Influence the Evaluations

When cultures or subcultures differ on any factor, it would be expected that differences in the evaluations would also be found on that factor. If gender and racial biases, positive or negative, exist in a society from which the students come, these same biases should appear in the evaluations. It would also be expected that instructors who share important cultural values with students would find it easier to obtain higher evaluations. Lazos (2012) reflected on this issue as it effects women and minority instructors. "The classroom is filled with positive and negative emotions. Students enter the classroom with unconscious stereotypes about the professor's race, ethnicity or accent, which in turn informs how the student perceives, listens, and reacts to the professor" (p. 184).

There Will Be an Interaction Between Social Class, Cultural, and Personal Factors

If a society puts more emphasis on female attractiveness than male attractiveness, then female instructors should benefit more from being physically attractive. If the students are sensitive to culturally "correct" bias and do not wish to appear "incorrect," they might emphasize male attractiveness while mitigating the impact of female characteristics (Hamermesh and Parker (2005). If a culture puts emphasis on females being more supportive and caring, then a female instructor would be expected to receive more benefit from being caring than a male instructor, or be punished more for not being caring (Sprague & Massoni, 2005). One study showed that simply reminding students of a culturally accepted norm could change the evaluations (see Peterson, Biederman, Ditonto, & Roe, 2019 for a fascinating example). In another experiment (Ewing, Stukas, & Sheehan, 2003), a male and a female instructor delivered either a "strong" or a "weak" lecture. In one group, the students believed the lecturer was a gay man and that the second lecturer was a lesbian. The second group received no gender-orientation information. Contrary to the study's predictions, weak lectures by gay male and lesbian lecturers were rated more positively than when no gender orientation was known. The paper suggested, "the possibility that students might moderate their ratings to avoid discriminating against gay and lesbian lecturers" (p. 569). As Valsan and Sproule (2008) state, "Current research shows that, at most, teaching scores reveal the extent to which the professor is able to connect to the students' cultural beliefs and live up to their expectations" (p. 940).

Instruction Takes Place in a Specific Environment Which Has Both Personal and Cultural Meaning for Students

What are students' expectations of a higher education? It has been hypothesized, for example, that students have a schema of how professors should look and act (Chisholm, 1977; Yermack & Forsyth, 2016). Further, it has been claimed that the instructor's effect on students depends more on their perception of the instructor than it does on the instructor's expertise (Hattie, 2009; Marsh & Bailey, 1993). In addition, do students see themselves as customers of the university, or do they accept the role of products and partners (Bunce, Baird, & Jones, 2017)?

In almost all cases, high grades are desirable to students. Our society sees positive grades as an indication of achievement, both personally and professionally, and individuals and parents display them with pride. It is also known that people update and modify their beliefs more if information is consistent with desired outcomes (Tappin, van der Leer, & McKay, 2017). The beliefs themselves, thus modified, need not be objectively correct. As Pollio and Beck (2016) observed when looking at the relationship between learning and grades, "the appearance of achievement becomes more important than the achievement itself" (p. 84). Grades, then, should be associated with SET. The arguments to explain away this connection strike this writer as artificial and contrived. Of course, the students who learn the most will receive the highest grades on average, but this is like saying hot days have higher temperatures, so higher temperatures must be the cause of hot days.

Educational expectations would explain a number of paradoxes in SET usage. It would, for example, predict why an odd and eccentric professor may be popular at a small private school and a pariah at a regional, public university.

The Likability Hypothesis Explains Why Reliability and Validity Measures Have Been Found to Differ So Radically in SET

While there is a general consensus of what people like and want, what will be expressed by individuals at any given time will vary dramatically. One student may find a class fascinating and want to learn as much as possible, while another may only want to check off the box, get a grade which does little damage to the ego, and get out of there. With no change whatsoever in anything the instructor did or did not do, what students like about a class or the instructor will coincide on some issues and be substantially different on others. The SET score is the average effect of all factors. If more students wanted to learn than just get by, there would be a positive association between learning and the evaluations; if the majority of students simply wanted to check off the box, or found learning the material too time-consuming, difficult, or ego-threatening, then there would be no association (or a negative one) found between learning and SET.

> An interesting model for the likability hypothesis would be the satisfaction measures published on travel sites. Hotel ratings, for example, are requested from people who spent a night or more at the hotel. The ratings will typically vary across the entire range of the evaluation instrument. A highly rated hotel will still usually have a guest who gives it the lowest rating, and no matter how poor a hotel may be, given enough evaluations, someone will rate it highly. Researchers in the hospitality industry maintain a guest's experience is not limited to what a hotel offers, but instead is co-created by both the service provider and the guest. Satisfaction can be seen as the guest's evaluation of their experience through their interaction with services rather than a direct measure of the service itself (Xiang, Schwartz, Gerder, & Uysal, 2015).

Pedagogic Idealism

Unless SET is seen as a customer satisfaction survey, the likability hypothesis separates the evaluations from a need for pedagogic idealism. It avoids problematic aspects of the SET paradigm, which for decades required explanations of both research and application to conform to appropriate ideology, even when, in many cases, it was not warranted by research or practical experience. It allows contradictions to be acknowledged along with centuries of experience, which, for example, would suggest that, on occasion, the most-effective student experiences (best lessons) come from thoroughly disliked instructors.

New Definition

The likability hypothesis allows us finally to give a definition for "good" or "effective" teaching.

> *Effective Teaching, as Measured by SET, is an Imperfect Assessment of Student Perceptions in an Instructional Environment*

Summary

1. SET does not directly measure the instructor or the instructor's instruction. In fact, SET does not require these to be measured at all.
2. The SET process attempts to measure student perceptions without ironically attempting to measure student behavior.
3. The SET scores an instructor receives from a class is an averaging measure of student perceptions filtered through an assessment instrument.
4. Finding negative or distracting elements within SET does not mean the instruments are somehow contaminated or erroneous.
5. SET is measuring what it was inadvertently designed to measure – imperfect assessments of student perceptions of an undefined hypothetical construct. From any philosophical, methodological, or mathematical approach, we can do no better than that.

Notes

1. TedGlobal2009, Optical illusions shows how we see. Retrieved from www.ted.com/talks/beau_lotto_optical_illusions_show_how_we_see?language=en
2. Unknown writer in AAUP Bulletin. Retrieved from www.aaup.org/article/social-class-and-college-readiness#.W3SEDs5Kjcu.

References

Berk, R. A. (2013). *Top 10 flashpoints in student ratings and the evaluation of teaching.* Sterling VA: Stylus.

Bunce, L., Baird, A., & Jones, S. (2017). The student-as-consumer approach to higher education and its effects on academic performance. *Studies in Higher Education, 42*(11), 1958–1978. https://doi.org/10.1080/03075079.2015.1127908

Cahoone, L. (2010). The modern intellectual tradition: From Descartes to Derrida. *The Great Courses* (Course No. 4790). Chantilly, VA: The Great Courses.

Chisholm, M. G. (1977). Student evaluation: The red herring of the decade. *Journal of Chemical Education, 54*(1), 22–23. Retrieved from https://pubs.acs.org/doi/pdf/10.1021/ed054p22

DeAngelis, T. (2015). Class differences. *American Psychological Association Monitor on Psychology, 46*(2), 62.

Ewing, V. L., Stukas, A. A., & Sheehan, E. P. (2003). Student prejudice against gay male and lesbian lecturers. *The Journal of Social Psychology, 143*(5), 569–579. https://doi.org/10.1080/00224540309598464

Hamermesh, D. S., & Parker, A. M. (2005). Beauty in the classroom: Professors' pulchritude and putative pedagogical productivity. *Economics of Education Review, 24*(4), 369–376. https://doi.org/10.1016/j.econedurev.2004.07.013

Hativa, N. (2014). *Student rating of instruction: Recognizing efective teacher* (2nd ed.). eBook: Oron Publications.

Hattie, J. (2009). *Visable learning: A synthesis of over 800 meta-analyses relating to achievement*. New York: Routledge. As referenced by: Yermack, J., & Forsyth, D. R. (2016). Students' implicit theories of university professors. *Scholarship of Teaching and Learning in Psychology, 2*(3), 169–178. https://doi.org/10.1037/stl0000067

Lazos, S. R. (2012). Are students teaching evaluations holding back women and minorities? The perils of "Doing" gender and race in the classroom. In G. Gutierrez Muhs, Y. F. Niemann, C. G. Gonzalez, & A. P. Harris (Eds.), *Presumed incompetent: The intersections of race and class for women in academia*. Utah State University Press, University Press of Colorado. Retrieved from www.jstor.org/stable/j.ctt4cgr3k.19

Marsh, H. W., & Bailey, M. (1993). Multidimensional students' evaluations of teaching effectiveness. *The Journal of Higher Education, 64*(1), 1–18. https://doi.org/10.1080/00221546.1993.11778406

Peterson, D. A. M., Biederman, L. A., Ditonto, T. M., & Roe, K. (2019). Mitigating gender bias in student evaluation of teaching. *PLoS One, 14*(5), e0216241. http://doi.org/10.137/Journal.pone0216241

Pollio, H. R., & Beck, H. P. (2016). When the tail wags the dog: Perceptions of learning and grade orientation in, and by, contemporary students and faculty. *The Journal of Higher Education, 71*(1), 84–102. https://doi.org/10.1080/00221546.2000.11780817

Sprague, J., & Massoni, K. (2005). Student evaluations and gendered expectations: What we can't count can hurt us. *Sex Roles, 53*(11/12), 779–799. https://doi.org/10.1007/s11199-005-8292-4

Tappin, B. M., van der Leer, L., & McKay, R. T. (2017). The heart trumps the head: Desirability bias in political belief revision. *Journal of Experimental Psychology: General, 146*(8), 1143–1149. http://dx.doi.org/10.1037/xge0000298

Valsan, C., & Sproule, R. (2008). The invisible hands behind the student evaluation of teaching: The rise of the new managerial elite in the governance of higher education. *Journal of Economic Issues, 42*(4), 939–958. https://doi.org/10.1080/00213624.2008.11507197

Xiang, Z., Schwartz, Z., Gerder, J. H., & Uysal, M. (2015). What can big data and text analytics tell us about hotel guest experience and satisfaction? *International Journal of Hospitality Management*, *44*, 120–130. https://doi.org/10.1016/j.ijhm.2014.10.013

Yermack, J., & Forsyth, D. R. (2016). Students' implicit theories of university professors. *Scholarship of Teaching and Learning in Psychology*, *2*(3), 169–178. https://doi.org/10.1037/stl0000067

15 Conclusion and Recommendations – the Future of SET

Is There a Bottom Line?

Flawed Paradigm

The study of the SET process provides a fascinating look into assessment and the problems and consequences of a widely used instrument. Without a doubt, the process has had some positive benefits. Instructors have been held more responsible for their behavior and the content of their classes. Student input into their own education is a valuable goal, and it is this writer's opinion that institutions of higher learning are more welcoming and student-oriented than ever before.

Nevertheless, the current SET process presents a seriously flawed paradigm.

Given the prestige of certain researchers and the careful analyses of the SET process that created their reputations, it was once reasonable to defend the evaluations, but given the evidence from the past 20 to 25 years, this optimism no longer appears to be justified. In fact, why SET is still so widely defended has become the question remaining to be investigated. The irony, given these results, is how little impact the research has had on the actual utilization of the evaluations. It would be easy to assume, at this point, that SET has become more of an ideological and bureaucratic necessity than an evidence-driven one.

Unanswered Question

Given the near universal applications of SET over decades, a concluding question that ought to be asked of the SET process remains largely unaddressed.

What Has Been the Result of Our Experience With Student Evaluation of Teaching?

Are students better educated? Are instructors teaching at a higher level? Has education been improved? Has society benefited?

> The universal application of SET has led to some normative tradeoffs. Long ago, Chisholm (1977, p. 23) wrote, "The atrocious teacher has indeed vanished, but so also has the brilliant eccentric."

Although it is difficult to isolate the influence of the SET process from other factors, the evaluations have coexisted with significant changes in higher education. While some sources have shown a positive improvement in instruction (Murray, 1997), and some increases in the importance placed on student perceptions (Palermo, 2013), the increased use of SET has occurred in conjunction with what many believe to be an educational decline (see Arum & Roska, 2011; Babcock & Marks, 2010; Flinn & Crumbley, 2009; Hebel, 2006; Jones, 2018; Willingham, 2016; Wines & Lau, 2006).

After almost 30 years of researching the evaluation instruments, this writer has come to believe student perceptions of teaching have a legitimate, but limited, function. The use of SET information must be held to a very high standard. When evaluations are used by virtually all schools, consume considerable resources, and constitute a major (and in some cases, the only) measure of faculty instructional competency, more than good faith, theory, or administrative necessity is warranted.

References

Arum, R., & Roska, J. (2011, January 18). Are undergraduates actually learning anything? *The Chronicle of Higher Education, Commentary*. Retrieved from http://chronicle.com/article/Are-Undergraduates-Actually/125979

Babcock, P. S., & Marks, M. (2010, April). *The falling time cost of college: Evidence from half a century of time use data* (NBER Working Paper, No. 15954). Retrieved from www.mitpressjournals.org/doi/abs/10.1162/REST_a_00093

Chisholm, M. G. (1977). Student evaluation: The red herring of the decade. *Journal of Chemical Education, 54*(1), 22–23. Retrieved from https://pubs.acs.org/doi/pdf/10.1021/ed054p22

Flinn, R. E., & Crumbly, D. L. (2009). *Measure learning rather than satisfaction in higher education.* Sarasota, FL: American Accounting Association.

Hebel, S. (2006, September 15). Report card on colleges finds US is slipping: Progress in America slows as it is "Outperformed by many other countries". *Chronicle of Higher Education,* A1, A21–A24. Retrieved from www.chronicle.com/article/Report-Card-on-Colleges-Finds/3508

Jones, J. M. (2018, October 9). Confidence in higher education: Down since 2015. *Gallup Blog.* Retrieved from https://news.gallup.com/opinion/gallup/242441/confidence-higher-education-down-2015.aspx

Murray, H. G. (1997). Does evaluation of teaching lead to improvements of teaching? *International Journal for Academic Development, 2*(1), 8–23. https://doi.org/10.1080/1360144970020102

Palermo, J. (2013). Linking student evaluations to institutional goals: A change story. *Assessment & Evaluation in Higher Education, 38*(2), 211–223. https://doi.org/10.1080/02602938.2011.618880

Willingham, D. (2016, September 14). A telling experiment reveals a big problem among college students: They don't know how to study (As told by Valerie Strauss). *The Washington Post.* Retrieved from www.washingtonpost.com/news/answer-sheet/wp/2016/09/14/a-telling-experiment-reveals-a-big-problem-among-college-students-they-dont-know-how-to-study/?utm_term=.02d8efb3b5ae

Wines, W. A., & Lau, T. J. (2006). Article: Observations on the folly of using student evaluations of college teaching for faculty evaluation, pay, and retention decisions and its implication for academic freedom. *William and Mary Journal of Women and the Law, 13*(1), Article 4. Retrieved from http://scholarship.law.wm.edu/wmjowl/vol13/iss1/4

Index

Abel, Millicent H. 18
Adams, Michael 115
Adrian, C. Mitchell 26
Aleamoni, Lawrence M. 124
Ambady, Nalini 32
Appleton-Knapp, Sara L. 68
attribution and validity 106–107

Bacon, Donald R. 50
Bauer, Kristina N. 57
Beck, Hall P. 139
Becker, William E. 77
Bennett, Sheila K. 15
Benz, Carolyn R. 107
Beran, Tanya N. 93
Berk, Ronald A. 134
Bermann, Barbara R. 92, 113
Beyer, Denise 38
Blatt, Sidney J. 107
Boring, Anne 18
Brockx, Bert 76
Brown, Kenneth G. 57
Brown, Tom J. 82

Campbell's Law 96
Carle, Adam C. 75
Carlozzi, Michael 7–8
Carpenter, Shana K. 35
Cashin, William 6, 37, 50, 51, 94, 113
Cashin, William E. 6, 37, 50, 94, 113
Centra, John A. 75, 114
Ching, Gregory 69
Chisholm, Mary G. 145
Chonko, Lawrence B. 88
Chung, Choi-Man 52
Churchill, Gilbert A. 82

Clayson, Dennis E. 25–26, 39, 51, 76, 89, 91
Cnudde, Kelsey 6
Coe, Robert 96
Cohen, Peter A. 52, 64, 75, 104
concurrent validity 89, 90
construct validity 90
Cronbach, Lee 83, 84, 85
Crumbley, Donald L. 58
Culver, Steven 55
customers as students: happiness of students as main objective 130–131; as a modern idea 6; products and partners, students accepting the role of 93–94, 139; SET as providing a customer-like relationship with a school 91; student satisfaction component to instruction 26, 83, 94, 104

deductive and inductive knowledge, distinguishing between 114
Delucchi, Michael 66
diagnostic validity 104
divergent validity 90, 96, 116, 126
Dodeen, Hamzeh 84
Dowell, David A. 65
Dr. Fox effect 34–36, 125, 138

Edmundson, Mark 95
Ely, Katherine 57
Emery, Charles R. 46
English, Taylor 32
evaluation instruments: class averages, reliability of 82; Finkelstein on the validity of 117; growing use

of evaluation systems 3–4; hotel ratings example 140; instruction not affected by 75; as legitimate but limited 131, 145; methodological restraints, as hampered by 106; personality inventory, replacing with 28; reliability of instruments without validity 84, 125; subjectivity in evaluation interpretations 112; tenure decisions, used to determine 67; validity of an instrument as goal dependent 87

face validity 88
factor analysis of instructor characteristics 89
Feistauer, Daniela 114
Feldman, Kenneth A. 6, 24, 37, 82
Finkelstein, Martin J. 117
Fliedner, Eugene 58
Flinn, Ronald E. 89
Follman, John 83
Foote, David A. 26
formative function 103, 104, 134
Franklin, Jessica 35, 113
Freedman, Richard D. 55

gender effects on evaluation: bias by gender of instructor and student 14; emotional impact of reviews on female instructors 19; gender bias assertions 13, 95; language bias 16–18; number of points on a scale, gendered responses to 108; unequal application of gendered expectations 15, 38; violation of norms, women instructors punished more for 55
Gillmore, Gerald M. 50, 52, 54, 83
good or effective teaching: commonalities between students, effect on assessment 137; contamination of intervening variables 8, 90, 123; defining 141; faculty research, no effect on student evaluations 115; gender bias in instructor assessment 94, 127–128; grades received as influencing evaluation 52; halo effect and 31–32; institutions not identifying or explaining 107; instructor experience as a negative factor in evaluation 38; learning, assumed to be related to 64, 106, 125; likable traits of instructor as the substance of 128; as mind and culturally dependent 91, 136; SET, considering as a valid measure of teaching 9, 88, 124; in specific disciplines 93; utilitarian reasons for accepting evaluations 130; as whatever the students say it is 2
grades: in Air Force Academy study 67; appearance of achievement, importance of 139; five theories on grade relationships to SET 53–54; grade-evaluation relationship as gendered 55; grading-leniency effect on evaluations 52; grading standards and student evaluations 51, 58, 125; higher student grades link to higher teacher evaluations 15, 113; instructor attractiveness, impact on student rating of grades 33; learning as measured by grades over time 68; of likable instructors 131; rigor-grade-evaluation association, lack of modern data on 49; teaching evaluation, student GPAs not affecting 56–57
Gray, Mary 92, 113
Greenwald, Anthony G. 50, 52, 54, 90
Grimes, Paul W. 107
Grobe, Jennifer L. 77
Gurung, Regan A. R. 33

Haley, Debra A. 51, 76, 89, 91
halo effect: attractiveness halo 32, 33; evaluations affected by 45, 90, 138; grade-workload-difficulty correlation 55; objective student learning, not appearing to influence 39
Hamermesh, Daniel S. 33
Harmon, Susan K. 26
Hau, Kit-Tai 52
Hayes, Andrew F. 82
Henslee, Amber M. 32
Hocevar, Dennis 82
Hocutt, Max 94
homoscedasticity 108
Hornstein, Henry A. 106
House, Deanna 16
Howard, Caroline 96
Hoyt, Donald P. 93, 106, 110

instructional improvement: external feedback 76–77, 78; formative function of 104; improvement hypothesis 74–75; Israeli study on 50
instructor morale 19, 96
Irons, Jessica 32

Johnson, Valen 51, 55, 67, 113

Kanazawa, Satoshi 33
Keeley, Jared W. 32
Kornell, Nate 35
Kors, Alan Charles 120
Kovard, Jody 33
Krentler, Kathleen A. 68
Krippendorff, Klaus 82, 84
Kunda, Ziva 95

Langbein, Laura I. 83
Lantos, Geoffrey P. 26
Lau, Terence J. 116
Lazos, Sylvia R. 13, 138
learning: attractiveness of instructor correlated with 33; complicating variables 68–69; deep learning 67–68, 70; defining 65; Dr. Fox study, perceived learning in 34, 36; gender, learning expectations of instructors based on 15, 38; grades, assuming correlation to 50, 54, 57; halo effects on objective student learning 39; lecture fluency, low impact on information learned 35; likability and 126–127; meta-analysis on 8; personality variables in perception of learning 25; political orientation, effect on learning 37, 39; rigor, assuming correlation with 2, 51; SET not an assessment of 36, 66–67, 70–71, 126, 127; teacher effectiveness and student learning 64; validity and 106
Lee, Eun-Joo 93
likability hypothesis: administrative reaffirmation of theory 131; Aristotle quote as reinforcing hypothesis 129; conclusion of SET as a measure of students 130, 134, 135; contradictions in research as explained by 132; high association between likability and SET 114;

justifications and implications of theory 133; likability and learning 126–127; pedagogic idealism and 140–141; rejections of theory 123–124; research implications 127–128, 137–140
Lin, Tin-Chun 55
Linask, Maia 74
Linse, Angela R. 70
Lotto, Beau 137

Machina, Kenton 117
main effects (global differences) 13, 14, 19, 50–51
Marks, Ronald B. 51, 90
Marsh, Herbert: defense of SET research findings 6, 52, 96, 112; Dr. Fox study, critique of methodological weaknesses in 34–35; feedback, on the effectiveness of 76; Feldman study, review of 82; on inappropriate use of individual student data 83; leniency, on class as the appropriate case for 54, 57; SEEQ form, as creator of 3
Mayo, Donna T. 26
measurement concerns 107–108
Meltzer, Andrea L. 18
Mengel, Friederike 18
Miles, Patti 16
Millea, Meghan 107
Miron, Mordechai 75–76
Monks, James 74
Monteiro, Heather 38
Moore, Pat 89, 113
Morley, Donald D. 84
Mortelmans, Dimitri 76
motivation hypothesis 54
Mullaney, Kellie M. 35
Murray, Harry G. 35, 114

Neal, Jones A. 65
Novotny, Jenny 50

objectivity, limits of 134–135
Onwuegbuzie, Anthony J. 89

Page, Colin F. 27, 123–24, 129
Parker, Amy M. 33
pedagogic idealism 140–141
Pelowski, Susan 66

Penny, Angela R. 96
perception, nature of 135–136
personality-evaluation association: business students study regarding 25; classroom behaviors vs. personality traits 114; cross-lagged model, measurements done by 26; high relation of personality to SET 23, 53; instructor self-perception of personality 24, 27, 28, 125; personality and teaching, differentiating between 124; of teachers rated best/worst 91, 95
Phelps, Lonnie D. 26
physical attractiveness, bias of: attractiveness halo 32, 33; evaluations, influence on 31, 34, 39; female instructor skill as linked to attractiveness 16, 138; "hotness" correlation 33, 45; performance, no significant impact on 115
Plato and analogy of the cave 135
political orientation influence on SET 36–37, 39
Pollio, Howard R. 139
popular professors 123
predictive validity 89
purposeful misreporting 46, 47, 125

RateMyProfessors.com 8, 16–17, 33, 89, 95
reciprocity hypothesis 54–56, 57, 58
reliability of student evaluations: between-class reliability 83; definition of reliability 81–82; inter-rater reliability 84, 85, 125; likability hypothesis, applying to reliability measures 140; stability of SET results as argument for reliability 77, 82
Reynolds, David V. 46
Richter, Tobias 114
rigor: cultural biases in reaction to 15; defining 50; evaluations as generally unrelated to 125; gender expectations for rigorous coursework 19; historical developments in 52–53; learning, assumed connection with 2, 51; performance, no significant impact on 115; rigor-grade-evaluation association 49, 57, 58

Roche, Lawrence A. 6, 52, 54, 83
Rodin, Burton 65
Rodin, Miriam 35
Rosenthal, Robert 32

Scaling Concerns 107–108
Schmidt, Peter 16–17, 18
Seldin, Peter 4
Sepehri, Mohamad 115
Sheffet, Mary J. 25–26
Siguaw, Judy A. 70
Simpson, Penny M. 70
Sinclair, Lisa 95
Sitzmann, Traci 57
Siu, Teresa L. 52
Smibert, Dylan 93
Smith, Calvin 76, 77
Spooren, Pieter 76
Sproule, Robert 45, 90, 139
Stake, Jeffrey E. 113
Stanfel, Larry E. 45
Stark, Philip 129
statistical concerns 107–108
stereotypes: Clayson study on 39; gender stereotypes 15, 16, 17, 18; social stereotypes and gender bias 19; unconscious stereotypes 138
student-as-thermometer model 136–137
student evaluation of teaching (SET): age/experience of instructor and 37–39; civil rights and diversity concerns 95–96; contamination concerns 8, 25, 123, 124, 127, 128, 132, 141; as demeaning to faculty 92; evaluations and the law 116–117; as a flawed paradigm 144; high standards, punishing instructors who maintain 50; honesty concerns 44–47; likability scale, producing 90, 91; Likert scale, making adjustments to 16; long-term consistency of evaluations 77, 82–84, 85; mean scores 19, 25, 127; ontological inconsistencies in interpretations 93–95; perceptual distortion as reflected in 130; physical and philosophical justification 135–137; psychological and perceptual justifications for 134–135; randomization and

evaluations in subsequent classes 68; repeated administrations of 76, 78; research implications 137–140; self-perpetuating consensus of early research 5–6; skewness of responses 57, 108; statistical discrimination theory, applying to scoring 18; strong opinions on 112–113, 118; tautological error in validation of SET responses 114–115, 127
Stumpf, Stephen A. 55
summative assessment: inappropriate assumptions and statistical analyses 108; of instructors in specific disciplines 93; likability hypothesis, acknowledging 131; mean scores, utilizing 127; SET as a primary summative agent, justification lacking for 105; summative agent bias 130; summative function 103, 104–105; summative validity 104; universal utilization of instruments 116; valid response rates for statistical acceptability 134

Tang, Terrill T-L 106–107
Tang, Thomas Li-Ping 106–107
teaching effectiveness hypothesis 53
temptations in data utilization 93
Theall, Michael 35, 113
Thorndike, Edward 31–32
Thornton, Barry 115

Totten, Jeffery W. 26
Trout, Paul 36
truthfulness of students 44–47, 113

utilitarian function 103, 104, 105
Uttl, Bob 6, 8, 93

validity: content validity 88–89, 96; convergent validity 90, 96, 124, 126; discriminant validity 19, 96, 116, 124, 126; logic and 113–115; nomological validity 91, 96; purpose and 103–105; reproducibility as most feasible test of 82; standard definition as lacking 87, 96, 105–106; types of validity 88–91; utilitarian validity 91, 92–96, 97; validity concerns 107–108
Valsan, Calin 139
Vespia, Kristin 33
Violato, Claudio 93

Ware, John E. 34–35
Watts, Michael 77
Weinberg, Bruce A. 69–70
White, Carmela A. 6
Wilford, Miko M. 35
Wilhelm, Wendy Bryce 51
Wilson, Janie H. 38
Wines, William A. 116
Woodruff, Thomas W. 107

For Product Safety Concerns and Information please contact our EU representative GPSR@taylorandfrancis.com
Taylor & Francis Verlag GmbH, Kaufingerstraße 24, 80331 München, Germany

www.ingramcontent.com/pod-product-compliance
Lightning Source LLC
Chambersburg PA
CBHW051748230426
43670CB00012B/2207